Alamo Village

ALSO BY JOHN FARKIS

*Not Thinkin'… Just Rememberin'…
The Making of John Wayne's* The Alamo

Alamo Village:
How a Texas Cattleman Brought Hollywood to the Old West

by

John Farkis

BearManor Media

2017

Alamo Village: How a Texas Cattleman Brought Hollywood to the Old West

© 2005, 2016 John Farkis

All rights reserved.

No part of this book may be reproduced in any form or by any means, electronic, mechanical, digital, photocopying or recording, except for inclusion in a review, without permission in writing from the publisher.

For information, address:

BearManor Media
P. O. Box 71426
Albany, GA 31708

bearmanormedia.com

Typesetting and layout by John Teehan

Published in the USA by BearManor Media

ISBN— 978-1-62933-090-7

Table of Contents

Acknowledgements vii

Foreword ix

Alamo Village: How a Texas Cattleman Brought
Hollywood to the Old West 1

Appendix A: Selected Alamo Village Buildings
Constructed in 1959 211

Appendix B: Composition and Construction
Method of Fort Clark/Bracketville Buildings
in 1959 219

Bibliography 237

Notes 245

Acknowledgements

The book that you are now holding was first published in 2005. During the last eleven years I've been able to uncover a great deal of new research which significantly changed many of my initial observations and comments. As a result, I have incorporated that information into this new, revised edition. In addition, I've also added extra content regarding the history of Fort Clark, Brackettville and the creation of Alamo Village. Along with those changes, I've also included over 222 new photographs, many of which have never been published before as well as several new interviews. Where applicable, I've added content from my last book, "Not Thinkin'…Just Rememberin'…" This book can now also serve as a tour guide to Alamo Village itself. For those fortunate enough to have visited the set, many "Then and Now" photographs will help identify exactly where specific scenes were filmed. And, if you weren't so lucky, the book should give you a good indication as to what it might have been like to be on location.

It almost goes without saying that this type of project is not the result of just a single person's effort. Although this book took much longer than I expected, I never failed to receive the support and encouragement from many individuals and organizations along the way. My deepest thanks and appreciations go out to Lisa Baehr (I know this project wasn't what you expected but you came through with flying colors), Frank Thompson, Ashley Ward III, Don Clark, Kevin Young, Ken Pruitt (absolutely awesome diorama), Bruce Winders, historian and curator at the Alamo, Elaine Davis (Library Director), Warren Stricker (Archivist), and Leslie Sitz Stapleton (Librarian) of the Daughters of the Republic of Texas Library, Laura Cantu (Library Assistant II) from the Institute of Texan Cultures, The Center of Archaeological Research University of Texan San Antonio, Wylie Simmons (vice-president of the Fort Clark Historical Society), Mary and Jose Hernandez III (thanks for the family photos), Bill Moody IV, Mark Lemon, and John J. Farkis (what a fantastic job!!). And finally, Virginia Shahan and Treva Schroeder from Alamo Village. Virginia, even though you are no longer with us, thank you for access to your files as well as your time and support. You were an extremely gracious lady. I regret that I never had a chance to meet Happy.

A special acknowledgement goes out to Richard Curilla at Alamo Village. Without his support, information, criticism and suggestions, this project never would have gotten off the ground. He never failed to answer any question no matter how mundane or inconsequential the subject matter. The after-hours private tour helped immeasurably in my understanding of not only the layout but also the history of Alamo Village. I have a newfound friend, which I value tremendously. Rich, I can't express how much I appreciate all that you have done for me. Someday you have to finish *your* book. I'd also like to thank Rick Hassler for performing the god-forsaken task of editor. I bet you didn't think it would take so much effort!

In particular, I would like to thank Alamo Village, Zack Davis, William Haenn, executive director Friends of the Fort Clark Historic District, Maurice Jones, Chris Hale, Kristi Hale and Ned Huthmacher for graciously allowing me to reprint photographs from their wonderful collections. Unless otherwise noted, all remaining photographs are from the author's collection. I have made every attempt to identify the source of each photograph. If I have failed to name someone and/or give them the appropriate credit, it was not intentional and I apologize.

Last and most important, I would like to thank my beautiful wife Jean for all her help, support and encouragement. You are my light and my love. You literally saved my life. I don't know what I would have done if I hadn't found you.

Foreword

When John Farkis showed up at Alamo Village over a decade ago, it was with a purpose. He was requesting access to the files of the late Happy Shahan in order to do research for an article he had a passion to write, as he explained it then, "about set construction techniques for John Wayne's movie *The Alamo*."

Now… There is a whole world of things one can write about a motion picture, particularly a very popular movie like this 1960, multi-million dollar epic. It has beautiful photography, wonderful scenery, excellent acting, a superb music score, lots of action–and John Wayne. This fellow, however, chose to write about wood, concrete and adobe. Of course we obliged him and took him to the files to see what he could find.

What he came up with was a lot more than he expected. He became fascinated with the whole story of how local rancher Happy Shahan had cajoled John Wayne over a two-and-a-half year period into shooting *The Alamo* on Happy's Southwest Texas ranch rather than in Mexico or Panama as Wayne had planned. Happy's way of summarizing it was, "John Wayne's plans changed." So did those of John Farkis.

For the next several years, John interviewed people in Texas and everywhere else regarding John Wayne, Happy Shahan and *The Alamo*. He made several trips to Alamo Village from Michigan to tour the sets with me and pick my brain about who, what, where, when and how. Having told the story to tourists on the streets of Alamo Village for many years, I was very happy that it was about to get accurately chronicled by this fine gentleman.

Of course, my years at Alamo Village (nearly thirty years) were the result of my own love for John Wayne's *The Alamo* and fascination with the making of the movie. I not only understood John Farkis' growing attachment to the story, I was thrilled by it. We became fast friends, and I was quite happy to be included in the process.

One of the first things I pointed out to John was that my narrative of these events was not mine at all. It was Happy's. I was simply repeating the story I heard him tell many times, and like all good storytellers, he improved it as time went by. In fact, I was shocked to discover by watching old videos of my own Alamo Village presentation in the years after Happy's death that even my story had changed a bit–that I had dropped parts that didn't seem too interesting to folks and colored other parts that I particularly liked. I guess my version is now more like folklore, accurate in general but not necessarily reliable as specific fact without cross-checking. John Farkis cross-checked! We both laughed many times about the differences he kept unearthing.

One of my favorites was why Happy Shahan decided to open the set to tourists after *The Alamo* premiered. During my tenure, Happy always said he had no intention of opening. He wished to continue doing movies on the set, if Hollywood was interested, but not tourism. It was a private ranch and he wanted to keep it that way. However, after the movie became so popular, people began cutting his fences to get in to see the sets. "In one week," he said, "I had three incidents of trespassing." What he then decided to do was hire a gateman and allow people in, using the admission charge to pay the gateman's salary. Then, in a short while, he realized that somebody was also needed down on the set "To watch things," and visitors needed someplace to get in out of the sun and catch a bite to eat, so he added a restaurant and staff–right in John Wayne's Cantina set. Soon came stagecoach rides and comedy gunfights and a shooting gallery so people wouldn't get bored while they visited–souvenir shops so they could go home with a memento. He intimated that all this was in answer to the needs of others.

In John's research, however, he found a transcript of a radio interview that Happy did while the sets were still being constructed–before one foot of film was shot–in which Happy said, "When John Wayne's done, I'm gonna turn it into a world class tourist attraction–call it Alamo Village. We'll have cowboys, Indians, stagecoaches, shootouts, good food…" The plan was there from the start.

In short, John Farkis turned out a masterpiece-in-the-raw with his self-published, paper-cover book *Alamo Village: How a Texas Cattleman Brought Hollywood to the Old West*. We were definitely pleased–and quite successful selling it in our gift shop. Virginia Shahan (Happy's late widow) was also very proud of it–and of John, whom she had really gotten to like. My only disappointment was that, as a home-brewed venture, it had a very limited market. Thus, I was exceedingly happy when John told me that the publisher of his unparalleled *Not Thinkin'… Just Rememberin'… The Making of John Wayne's The Alamo* had agreed to publish his Alamo Village book in a greatly expanded version.

Here is the book, and it is indeed "the rest of the story." It has always been a story that needed to be told, and it has now found its chronicler.

Richard L. Curilla
Brackettville, Texas
August 17, 2015

Alamo Village:
How a Texas Cattleman Brought Hollywood to the Old West

Many people familiar with John Wayne's version of "The Alamo" are aware that it was not filmed on a Hollywood soundstage or back lot, but rather on a set built on a ranch outside a small southwestern Texas town, where a replica of San Antonio and the Alamo mission compound of 1836 was constructed. How this site was selected and Alamo Village came to be, however, is the rest of the story…

Hot. *DAMN* hot. *TEXAS* hot!!!!! Not a cloud in the sky; a sky so blue it hurt your eyes just to look at it. Barely a breeze to cool you down. Wow! California boys were used to hot weather but nothing like this. The end of the day was approaching and Nate Edwards was hot, tired and more than that… he was worried. He had been out looking at potential properties all over Brackettville and the surrounding four-county area for the better part of a week and still hadn't come up with anything that would meet the requirements. Since Nate was production manager on the proposed film, Wayne told him in so many words, "Go to Texas, meet with Happy Shahan, and find the perfect site for *The Alamo*. And, don't come back until you do!"

Happy, so popular with his neighbors that he was elected mayor six times, was born James Tullis Shahan in an extremely small, two-room farmhouse on July 24, 1915, in the sleepy little east Texas town of Whitehouse to James William Shahan and Georgia Pearl Messer. His future bride, Virginia Francis Webb, was born seven months later, February 15, 1916, in Del Rio, Texas, to Elisha and Fanny Faye Adams Webb. The Webb family roots ran deep in Texas, dating back to the Texas Revolution. At the time of her birth, the Webbs owned a ranch in Edwards County and in 1927, along with daughters Virginia and Sara, moved from Rocksprings to Brackettville and bought another ranch in Kinney County, just forty-five miles from the Mexican border. Ambitious, creative, opportunistic, Elisha was the first to introduce sheep into the county as well as Angus and Longhorn cattle.

During the Roaring Twenties, a time of wealth, excess and wild speculation, the economy expanded at a rapid pace. The golden age of technological discovery saw the invention of radio, television and aviation. Investors were enamored with the possibility of unlimited returns on the stock market. But, there were also signs of impending trouble: high consumer debt, restrictive credit, low sales, a struggling agricultural sector and declining production. On October 29, 1929, it all came to a head and the market crashed. Over the following years, banks failed, businesses

*James Tullis "Happy" Shahan and Virginia Francis Webb Shahan.
Reprinted with the permission of Jamie Shahan Rains.*

closed and fifteen million employees were unemployed, including James William Shahan. When he arrived home after losing his job, he told his wife all the money they had was in his pocket. "Willie Honey, what are we going to do?" she cried. "Don't worry, Pearly Honey. We'll get by somehow." And, somehow they did. Even Happy pitched in, doing whatever he could to help his family make ends meet–cleaning chicken coops (not small ones, three hundred-foot-long ones), picking cotton and chopping wood, all while attending school. He must have acquired his ambition from his grandfather, Andrew Jackson Shahan. Andy, as he was called, came from Tennessee by way of the Carolinas and settled in Whitehouse where, in 1876, he established a trading post–Shahan's Grocery. He operated the local post office, farmed and ran cattle. People who knew Andy said Happy was more like his grandfather than anyone else.

While in high school, Happy became interested in basketball, a life-long love affair that eventually culminated in an athletic scholarship. In 1931, although the shortest guard in the lineup, his seven-man team won the Texas/Arkansas/Louisiana tri-state high school championship. Courted by universities all over Texas, Shahan enrolled at Tyler Junior College where he continued to succeed athletically; captain of his team and unanimous all-state guard. It was there where a sportswriter gave him the moniker "Happy" for his propensity to smile all the time. Upperclassmen treated the freshman to what was then known as hazing. "They whipped my butt, and I laughed at 'em," Happy said with a grin. After three years, with scholarship in hand, Happy moved on to Baylor where he met Virginia Webb. Recalled Happy, "I just saw her and I knew she was the girl for me. I told her (on the steps of her dormitory where she was sitting with a group of friends) that I was going to marry her, but she didn't believe me." Virginia quickly replied, "You're crazy!" "Well, do you have enough money to buy me a Coke?" asked Happy, "…and she knew I was crazy." During summers, while not in school, the East Texas Irishman worked as a roughneck at Humble Oil Co. and looked forward to a career in the oil business. In fact, when interviewed by the company president and asked what he wanted to do, Shahan replied, "I want your job."

Happy and Virginia were married in Waco on January 6, 1939, while still at Baylor, and the Webb ranch continued to prosper under Fanny even when Elisha passed away later that year, just five days after Happy and Virginia's first daughter Jamie was born. Unfortunately, Virginia wasn't able to attend her father's funeral as she was still in the hospital. However, Happy did and while there, his mother-in-law asked him about his future as the ranch duties were becoming too much for her; she wanted him to move to Brackettville and take over the ranch. "We're going to divide this property and we want to know what you want to do," she said. When Happy replied he wanted to work for Humble Oil, she said, "We'd like to have our daughter home. We'd like you to consider the offer." Happy needed time to mull over his options. "Well," Happy rationalized, "when I graduate I have a choice. I'm old enough to know I don't know ranching. But I'm old enough to know what I do know and what I want to do. I want to be the head man at Humble. (But,) I'll come down and work next summer if I can get a leave of absence." He did, he liked it: "I worked that summer and decided I could probably make it, but I wasn't ready." Shahan graduated from Baylor the next year with a B.A. degree in sociology and worked at the ranch another year and a half for a whopping $50 a month. The next year he got a 50 percent raise to… $75 a month![1]

When Fanny passed away, the Webb ranch was divided between Virginia and her sister Sara– ten thousand acres and half of Fanny's debt each. Recalled Happy, "When they divided (the ranch), I didn't even have enough money to pay me $50 a month, so I had to go hustle. (We) couldn't borrow any money because I didn't have any credit and we owed the debt but, finally, I was able to borrow some money from a bank in Uvalde. We inherited sixty-three cows and one thousand nine hundred sheep. But, no bulls so we traded for some." During the lean years, Happy would rope during the summer, take his winnings and buy traps that he used at night in the winter. He trapped for anything; fox, coons, ringtail. Then he'd sell the pelts. Between roping and trappings, he was able to pay the doctor's bills when Tulisha was born in 1941.

But that didn't last long. In 1944, Happy borrowed $50,000 and bought 10,000 lambs that he sold nine months later for $150,000! Then he bought out his sister-in-law's ranch and Angus herd, went into the registered Angus business and showed cattle. In 1946, he moved from the ranch into town so his children could go to school, and he built a store–Shaker Feed and Lumber. A regular jack-of-all trades, he had been a boxer, lampshade salesman, singer, drummer and hat blocker and by 1950, he was worth over $2 million, but he wasn't finished yet. That year, he purchased a building in La Pryor, Texas, and manufactured Wintergarden PVM (protein, vitamins and minerals), a livestock supplement. Little did he know that a drought of biblical proportions was on the horizon. By the end of 1957, 244 of 254 Texas counties had been declared as federal disaster areas; almost 100,000 farms and ranches went under and agricultural losses were estimated to be in excess of those experienced during the 1930s Dust Bowl. There were no ponds or tanks to hold water–creeks dried up. Schools were cancelled due to lack of this precious commodity. Bridges were closed when they became too dangerous to use. So many Texans were forced off the land the state was permanently transformed from rural to urban status. Some ranchers sold off or slaughtered their cattle, others traveled hundreds of miles in search of grass to feed their livestock. Shahan was no different.[2]

Shahan wearing his favorite cavalry hat in front of the Alamo chapel at Alamo Village.

In 1950, Happy was deep into the registered cattle business; buying high, selling even higher. He once bought a nineteen-year-old Angus heifer and paid $1,900 for her. She calved for the next five years and the first calf brought in $6,000. Another $8,000 heifer brought in $11,000 with her first two calves. Not a bad investment. But, nothing could offset the effects of the drought. "In 1951 I didn't owe a man a dime," bragged Shahan. "Twenty-two thousand acres under fence, leased and owned, fully stocked, money in the bank. By the end of 1955, I owed a half a million dollars. The drought, it got to where it cost me $10,000 to $15,000 every month just (for) feed. I'd have been better off if I had sold my cattle but it was too late then. But I wanted to save my herd." He went to East Texas where the drought wasn't so severe and bought eleven hundred acres. "I bought some land. I wanted to save my cows 'cause I knew some day it'd rain here."

Donating his time, hard work, talent, and finances for civic and community projects, Happy was a promoter of many things he truly believed in. "When you decide to live in a place, you do what you can about building it," he explained. He would do whatever he could to help attract additional business to the area. Honest and a man of his word, he would honor a contract written on a napkin and shake hands. After he moved from the ranch back into town, he served on the city council and the school board. Eventually, he finally became mayor of Brackettville. Virginia recalled Happy wanted that job in the mid-1940s when the decommissioned army base was offered to the city for "$1 and other valuable considerations." The government initially offered to sell the property to the county, which wasn't a bad idea as the local commissioners thought it could be used for a military academy or woolen scouring plant. One representative traveled several times to Washington, D.C. to work out the details but, upon his return, the county changed its mind.

Spring Street, Brackettville, 1935. The Petersen & Company building is on the left. A right turn at the corner on N. Ann Street will take you out to Alamo Village.

The First State Bank of Brackettville, located at the corner of North, Spring, and Ann Streets, also known as "Five Points." Las Moras Mountain and the new Kinney County Court House can be seen in the background, c. 1920s.

The fort was then offered to the city with the same results: an initial favorable response, but then rejection. After the fort was officially deactivated in 1946, it was sold for salvage to the Texas Railway Equipment Company in Houston, a subsidiary of Brown & Root. Happy knew of rumored injustices going on in Brackettville and wanted to put the town on the map. By being mayor, he could lead the community, instead of asking someone who wasn't imaginative enough to lead.[3]

By 1950, Brackettville had lost 40 percent of its population because of the base closure. "We got to looking for all the things that we could do to make our town more profitable and bring in industry," said Happy. "And we found that we could make bricks but we didn't have a half a million dollars to go into the brick business. We found out we could do a lot of things but it took money." As mayor, he was responsible for the well-being of the community but wasn't being too successful. "Things got a little tough (in Brackettville)," admitted Happy. "I was looking for things to bring the economy back. One night it just came to me–to make Western movies." Left with no other choice, the tall, lean, bespectacled rancher stood up at a town meeting one night and asked for silence. He needed to say what was on his mind. After the crowd quieted down, he made his pitch. "Why don't we try to make Western movies here?" he suggested. "They make them in Monument Valley and around Tucson and the ranchers always make money. Why not here?" He didn't know anything about the film industry, although in the 1940s he had made a few beer commercials. But he knew it would be profitable if the town could attract filmmakers. (He once said he became interested in films as a kid when he sold popcorn and peanuts between reels at the silent movie house. "I knew I'd be connected (in movies) when I was in third grade," he said. Asked by his teacher what he wanted to be when he grew up, he replied, "Well, I'm going to be an athlete, go to school; I'm going to be a rancher, going to make movies, going to be in the oil business and I'm going to be an entertainer.") The town elders threw out a challenge to make it work, and they laughed him out of the meeting. "They told me, 'Who in the world would want to come all the way out here, just to make a movie?' 'I don't know,' I replied. 'Who has asked them?' It kinda irritated me; I was humiliated, so to speak, for even having such an idea. I got it in my craw and decided I'd do it, God willing, or die trying." Earlier he had had the exact same conversation with best friend Bill Moody while the two were out riding horses. "I asked why would they come to Brackettville when they have all this beautiful scenery with streams and pines in Wyoming and Utah?" said Happy. The mayor was always fond of saying, "I firmly believe that man can achieve whatever the mind can conceive." After the meeting, Happy went home and told his wife, "I think I'll go out to Hollywood and tell them that they should come here to make movies." When she asked if he had lost his mind, he shrugged and said, "No… I think I'll go out there."

Virginia didn't know why her husband thought the movie industry would save their town. She thought a film was made in the area way back in the 1910s but couldn't be sure. Perhaps someone may have suggested the idea to Happy, or maybe he recalled that there were scores of silent movies made in and around Fort Clark/Brackettville and San Antonio between 1910 and 1929. Many famous silent-movie actors starred in Vitagraph films such as *The West Wind*, *Breaking In*, and *Lifting the Ban of Coventry* including Darwin Karr, Ned Finley, Harry Northrup, Logan Paul, Eleanor Woodruff, Eulalie Jensen, Rose Tapley, Marion Henry, Jasper Ewing Brady and, of course, Lillian Walker. For the most part, the extras and many of the minor actors were drawn from the enlisted personnel of the Fourteenth U.S. Cavalry stationed at the fort.[4]

The region had everything necessary for Westerns: trees, desert, mountains and streams, limitless expanses of flat lands. Livestock. A local lumber mill to construct movie sets, qualified handymen to build them. An abundance of willing citizens to appear as extras. Even a local resort

Bluffs on the right bank of the West Nueces River on the L.L. Davis ranch northeast of the Shahan ranch. About 15 to 20 miles from Brackettville but only 7 miles on horseback from Alamo Village.

In a scene filmed but not used, Mexican horsemen are seen by peasant women washing their clothes in the rock-strewn creek bed in front of these bluffs.

One of three stock "tanks" on the Shahan ranch created for "The Alamo." Reprinted with the permission of Richard Curilla/Alamo Village.

complete with a spring-fed, three hundred-foot-long swimming pool and hundreds of rooms and cottages for the cast and crew to call home, at least for a while. And most importantly, it helped the local economy when it brought in badly needed income. During filming, craftsmen, carpenters, extras, teamsters, plumbers, and common laborers would all find work. With actors in town, spectators would come from miles around to watch the movie being filmed on location. Cafés, gas stations, hotels, motels, grocery stores, and restaurants would all see increases in business.

Some people scoffed at Shahan's idea, others thought it had merit, but in Virginia's words, "He was a dreamer and visionary." Of course, he was also aggressive, stubborn and hard-headed. Just because something had never been done before didn't mean it couldn't be. As Happy used to say, "This is the perfect spot for film production and I can make it happen; it's starting already."[5]

To understand the economic demise of Brackettville, one must explore the symbiotic relationship between the hamlet and its local army base. As one prospered, so did the other. Soldiers enhanced the collective wealth of the community; the town provided the activities a restless, weary trooper needed. And, to understand that, one needs to know the history of both the fort and village. Brackettville, a small community of less than 2,000 residents about 120 miles due west of San Antonio, was located in Kinney County, just east of the Rio Grande near the Texas border: greasewood flats and sagebrush, mesquite and cactus gardens in the south, the beginnings of the Texas Hill Country in the north, all threaded by spring-fed streams and creeks with such descriptive names as Arenosa (sandy), Perdido (lost), Isleta (islet), Salado (salty), Derramadero (spillway), and, of course, Pinto and Nueces (nuts). Due to the cooling waters of Las Moras (The Mulberries) Creek, the area was long favored by indigenous Coahuiltecan Indians, and later by Comanche, Apache and other tribes. Named by Spanish conquistadores for the trees that lined the banks, the spot became a welcome respite for travelers–a spot to quench their thirst and eliminate the dust. During the late 1700s and early 1800s, the spring was also a rest stop on the eastern branch of the Great Comanche War Trail, the warriors' annual migration from the buffalo-hunting grounds of the Great Plains to the Rio Grande. In 1832 English physician John Charles Beales secured over eight million acres worth of empresario contracts to settle 1,450 colonists between the Nueces and Rio Grande rivers. With the backing of the Rio Grande and Texas Land Company, sixty pioneers settled along the banks of Las Moras creek, a few miles south of the spring in a village known as Dolores, named after Beales' wife. Wrote one settler, "The stream of Las Moras is a very pretty one, about three yards across and averages at the present time, about two feet and a half in depth; the water is beautifully clear, and runs on a level with the surface of the 'bottoms.' It has several very pretty groves of timber, consisting principally of live and white oak, and elm. The 'bottoms' below the villa, for some miles, are very broad, and exceedingly rich; in some places, where the beavers have made dams, the water has spread over several acres in width, offering excellent rice grounds. The site of the Villa de Dolores, our new town, is upon the left bank of the stream, in a small grove of live oak and thick underwood; it rises gradually from the stream, leaving a small 'bottom' of beautiful land for gardens. On the opposite side of the stream is a small grove containing some pretty sticks of timber.

"This morning, Messrs. Power, Paulson, Soto, and myself, with the Mexican guard, made an excursion to the head of the stream. We passed over most beautiful lands for about eight miles, when we arrived at the springs. These form large pools of very clear water, in the midst of a large grove of very fine timber, consisting principally of live and white oak, elm, pecan, and hickory.

(Thermometer, 99° in the tent). This timber continues on both sides of the stream all the way down to the Villa. The springs are full of fish, and are crossed in various directions by beaver-dams. The magnolia and other beautiful shrubs were in full blossom; altogether forming one of the prettiest spots I have seen anywhere. After resting a short time in the shade, we proceeded on to a hill which rises from the middle of the plain, to the height of about six hundred feet. We mounted to the top of it, and beheld the country spread out before us like a map. We could distinctly see the hills which give origin to the Nueces and Rio Frio, to the E.N.E. of us; the Moras, our own stream, running nearly due south and west of us, the Piedras Pintas and Sequete. The hill is composed of a very compact dark granite, and a fine species of soft limestone. It is situated about four miles from the head waters of Las Moras, and twelve from our Villa. After making our observations, we returned to the Villa highly gratified with our excursion."

Unfortunately, despite the seemingly numerous advantages, the settlement failed to proper, in large part due to the relative skill levels of the colonists. The soil would not produce crops without irrigation, an expensive and difficult process. Drought and blighted crops led to disenchantment, followed by abandonment. With the approach of Santa Anna's army in 1836, the citizens scattered to the winds; sadly a wagon train was massacred by Indians on its way to safety in Matamoros. Though its buildings remained, Dolores was never reoccupied; as the buildings crumbled, it became a rendezvous point for traders, trappers and other frontiersmen.[6]

In the 1840s San Antonio merchants, looking for a way to increase local commerce, desperately needed a means to transport their goods from the city of Saint Anthony to El Paso and beyond to California. Assigned to explore a viable road, on February 24, 1849, Lt. William Henry Chase Whiting, accompanied by West Point classmate Richard Howard, Lt. William F. Smith, Policarpo Rodriguez, Delaware Indian scout Jack Hunter and fifteen intrepid men, set out to find such a way. Over the next three months, Whiting's party successfully traveled to El Paso and back, first taking a northern route, then returning through San Felipe Creek (later the location for Del Rio) and on to Las Moras Spring. Tucked away in a dense grove of pecans and mulberries, the area proved an ideal location. The previous year, Samuel Maverick, a member of the Texan forces that defeated the Mexican Army in 1835 and one of the original signers of the Texas Declaration of Independence, also recognized the benefits of the area and claimed the spring in his headright survey. Whiting recognized its military potential and upon his return recommended the spot as a site for a fort. Less than one week later, Smith, Howard and Rodriguez were once again on their way back to Las Moras, assisting Lt. Col. Joseph Johnson with a military train of almost 300 wagons, 2,500 animals, six companies of the Third Infantry under the command of Maj. Jefferson Van Horne, and a group of emigrants on their way to California. The following year Maj. John Sprague took a wagon train of 4,000 animals, 175 soldiers and 450 civilians over the same route.[7]

(The following describes the significance of site selection and is excerpted from the National Register of Historic Places, Nomination form for Fort Clark. Detailed building descriptions for both Fort Clark and Brackettville can be found in the appendix.)

"Texas experienced a period of rapid growth and settlement following its Revolution, which in the previously unsettled western and northern lands brought about conflicts between the white settlers and the native Indians, who were reluctant to relinquish their hunting grounds. Following two years of significant prosperity and consequent increased settlement, the latter part of 1838 and 1839 were marked by Indian hostilities which continued as the settlements expanded." In September 1849, the Texas State Gazette quoted a settler as saying, "I see that the Comanches (sic.) are still continuing their forays upon the Texas border, murdering and carrying off defenseless frontier settlers who had been granted protection… They must be pursued, hunted, run down, and killed–killed until they find we are in earnest… they must be beaten up in all their covers and harassed until they are brought to the knowledge of… the strength and resources of the United States." The form continued, "By 1850 west Texas was being opened up for the transport of commercial goods as well as immigration with several well-marked trails... The location of trade and immigration routes was dictated by access to water and topographical features, the knowledge of which aided the Indians in planning their attacks. The demands of frightened settlers plus the necessity of guarding stage passengers, freight drivers and the United States Mail compelled the federal Government to initiate defense measures in the form of manned forts along the travel routes of Anglos and Indians alike." As a result, Fort Clark was established at Las Mora Springs on June 20, 1852, by companies C and E of the First Infantry, under command of Major Joseph Hatch LaMotte, along with an advance and rear guard of the U. S. Mounted Rifles, a total of five officers and 109 enlisted men. Supposedly, Lt. Sells of California carried orders that indicated that they were to "Build a fort–Build it to last." *(According to Friends of Fort Clark Historical District executive director William Haenn, however, there is no evidence that a Lt. Sells was ever posted to Fort Clark during the period June 1852-February 1861. Only two officers with the surname "Sells" served in the U.S. Army from its organization, September 29, 1789 to March 2, 1903: David Miles Sells from Iowa and Elijah Sells from Ohio.)* Initially, the fort began as a cantonment or temporary garrison of tents and shelters. As the result of negotiations between Lt. Col. D.C. Tompkins and Samuel Maverick, the land the fort was eventually built on was leased to the government on July 30, 1852, for a period of twenty years. For the princely sum of $50 per month, paid quarterly, the army was granted sole use of an eight-mile tract of land varying one-and-one half miles to two miles in breadth along Las Moras Creek. The army also was given permission to take as much hay, timber, fuel and stone as necessary for its use. Maverick passed away on September 2, 1870. When the fort's initial lease expired, Maverick's widow Mary Ann renegotiated the terms, increasing the rent based on the value of additional structures and property improvements. Finally, in 1885, the government purchased 3,693.2 acres of land for $80,000. Some noted that the landscape had a healthy elevation with patches of chaparral interspersed throughout the region "which often give to the scene a curious and picturesque appearance. This chaparral consists of thickets of naked thorns of several species, so thick, tangled and impenetrable, as to laugh the best cultivated hedgerows to scorn… When these thickets are cleared away the ground is exceedingly fertile and easily tilled." Others were not as easily impressed. Brevet Second Lt. Zenas Bliss wrote, "…there is nothing but sand, cactus, dense chaparral and poor grass to the end of our journey." Along with mustangs, quail and "Jack-ass Rabbits."[8]

The fort had originally been named Fort Riley in honor of the First Infantry's commanding officer, but one month later, on July 15, 1852, at Riley's request, the name was changed to Fort Clark in honor of Major John B. Clark, an officer who had died, probably of non-battle-related causes, on August 23, 1847, at San Juan De Ulua during the Mexican War. (San Juan was a large complex of fortresses, prisons and a former palace on an island overlooking Veracruz.) In an inspection report written one year later on August 1, 1853, Col. W.G. Freeman noted that while the troops were still encamped in tents, "(the soldiers) are engaged in constructing quarters (some of which are nearly completed)." Constructed with local materials by enlisted men under the supervision of skilled craftsmen, these buildings are no longer standing, though it is believed they were the post hospital, bakery and guardhouse. The guardhouse was described as constructed "of stone with a good prison attached with 3 cells for solitary confinement, 1 general cell and 1 prison room," while the hospital was just a log building and a tent.[9]

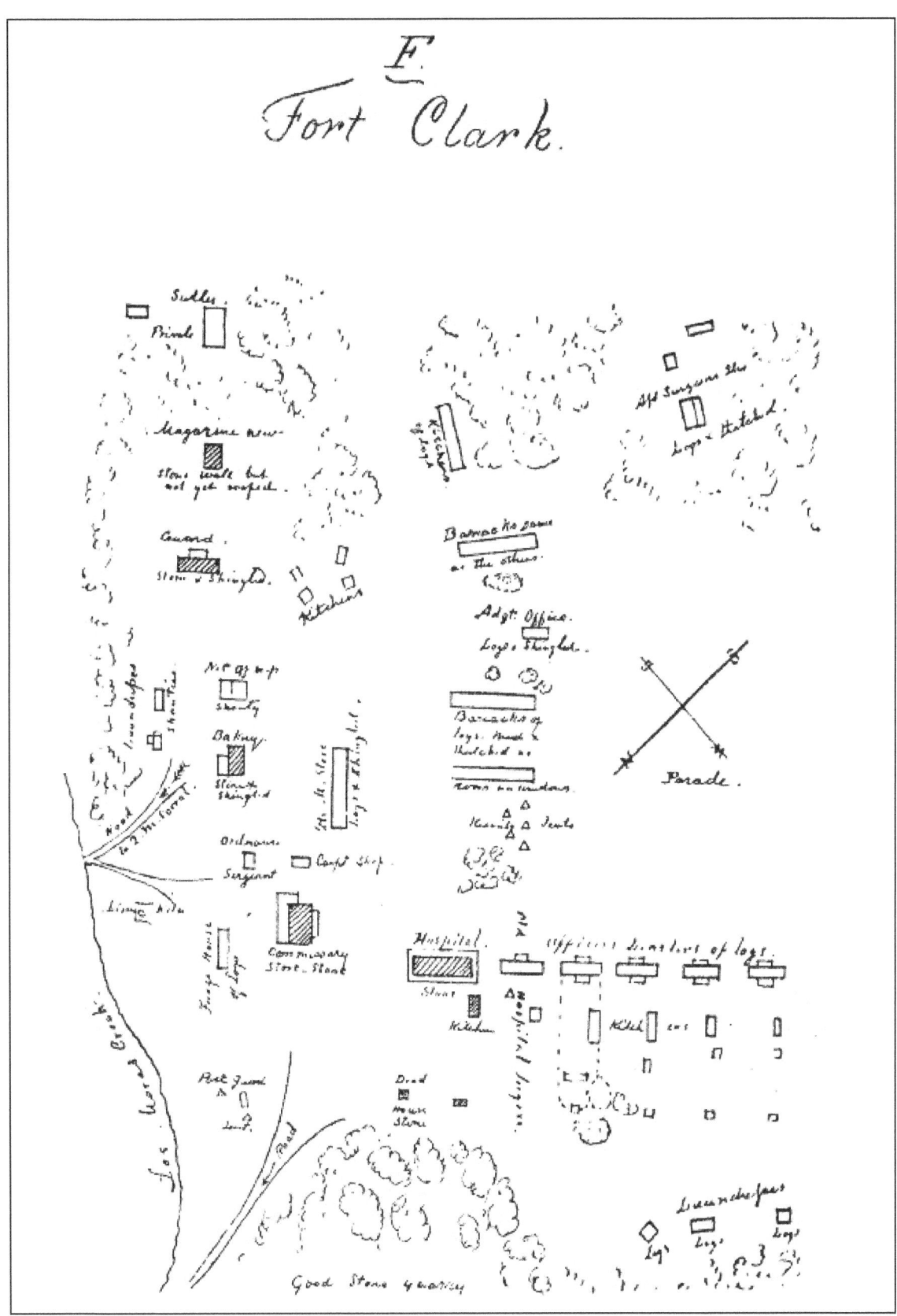

A map of Fort Clark sketched by Colonel Joseph K.F. Mansfield, 1856. Reprinted with the permission of William Haenn/Friends of the Fort Clark Historic District.

As was typical throughout the West, settlers would first build homes-the communities would soon follow. With the establishment of the fort, the neighboring hamlet of Las Moras was founded when Oscar Bernadotte Brackett, a San Antonio merchant, established a supply village to support the military. To honor its founder, the town's name was changed to Brackett in 1856. By the next year, the fort had added a headquarters building–constructed of rock from a nearby quarry–and a powder magazine. The post hospital was now built of stone with a kitchen and dead house. The magazine's walls had been erected but since there was an order *not* to use building materials without orders, construction was suspended without a roof. Ammunition thus was stored in the commissary. However, for the next twenty years, construction continued on the rest of the fort. Built in traditional military fashion, the post consisted of a row of barracks and officers' quarters separated by a parade ground, post headquarters, guard house, powder magazine, mess hall, commissary, hospital and stables. Tenth Infantry Second Lieutenant William Paulding described the post as "…one of great distances, three-quarters of a mile from the C.O.'s (Commanding Officer) quarters to the Q.M.'s (Quartermaster) store house and no shade…" Nine additional stone buildings were added to the post between 1873 and 1875; two-story officers' quarters with porch and back buildings–created on an L-shaped axis with six units on the long side of the "L" facing the parade ground, two units on the short side of the axis and a Commanding Officer's house. Each unit had a small yard enclosed by a white picket fence, with chinaberry trees, well-kept lawns and porches with Madeira vines.

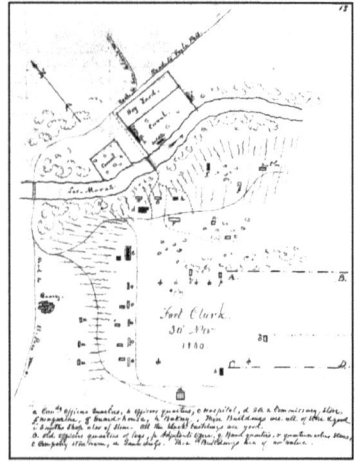

Fort Clark, November 30, 1860. Sketched by Colonel Joseph K.F. Mansfield. Reprinted with the permission of William Haenn/Friends of the Fort Clark Historic District.

The post footbridge over Las Moras Creek, c. 1896. This bridge was used by soldiers going back and forth to Brackettville. Note the turnstile on the Brackettville end of the bridge. Reprinted with the permission of William Haenn/Robert J. Sporleder Album, Fort Clark Historical Society.

In 1879, acting Assistant Surgeon Donald Jackson described the fort thusly: "There is no fort proper. The post is built on a quadrangle, one of whose sides, the northeast, run parallel to the Las Moras Creek, from which it is distance from 75 to 100 yards, and on an elevated ridge of nearly bare limestone rock, 40 or 50 feet above the level of the creek…"

"In the general barrack room, which is 100 by 20 feet, there are two doors and two windows in front, and one double door and two windows in the rear, with a large fireplace at each end. Ventilation is secured through the gable and ridge… There are no wash or bathrooms. Bedsteads are arranged in tiers, each 6 3/12 by 2 10/12 feet. There is a gun rack at one end and two shelves at the other, near the wall. These beds are placed at right angles to the wall, or across the barrack, in two rows. Bedsacks are filled with hay. Ordinarily each man has two blankets, of tolerably good quality.

"The water closets are of a temporary nature, built of wood, [and] situated about 150 yards from the barracks.

"A kitchen and mess-room of stockade, and shingled, has been erected for one of the barracks… There is also used as a kitchen and mess-room for one company, a stockade grass-covered building, formerly used as a traders' store… Married soldiers and laundresses are provided with small tents…

"Except for the commanding officer, who has two rooms, no officer has at present more than one, exclusive of kitchen. The officers and men not provided with quarters occupy tents.

"The privies are placed in the rear of the officers' quarters, at a distance of fifty yards, and are provided with portable boxes. There are no bath-rooms. Water is supplied from the spring by a wagon…

The Post Hospital consisting of a central two-story administrative building and two single-story patient wards, c. 1896. The white picket fence kept out the animals. Reprinted with the permission of William Haenn/Robert J. Sporleder Album, Fort Clark Historical Society.

"The guardhouse is a substantial stone building… and contains two rooms and four cells… The cells and prison-room are ventilated and lighted through grated holes high up in the wall, which are entirely too small, admitting an inadequate supply of air and light. There are no direct means of heating these cells or the general prisoners' room…

"The hospital requires a new roof, new joists under the porch, a few doors, and other general repairs…

"The post bakery is a substantial stone building… with shingled roof. In its rear is an oven capable of baking at one time 300 rations. There is neither chapel, laundry, nor schoolhouse at the post.

"The stable was formerly on the opposite side of the creek in the rear of the commissary and quartermaster's store-house, being a stockade shingle-roofed shed. It is very much dilapidated… A new stable, 200 by 30 feet, of boards, with shingle roof, has been lately finished, (and) situated 100 yards in the rear of the new barracks. It is divided into two rows of stalls…"

Brevet Lt. Col. H.C. Corbin added that the post's storehouse occupied two stories, one for the quartermaster and commissary, and one for the sales room. An attached stone building served as both a carpenter's shop and granary, with a three thousand bushel capacity.[10]

While the post expanded, so did the town, albeit in an uncontrolled and disorganized fashion. In November 1860, Col. Joseph K.F. Mansfield inspected Fort Clark and reported that to the east of Las Moras Creek, "…a village of trading stores has been put up… to the number of 5 or 6 & some hackalls & the stage station is there." By 1868 the village consisted of a mere ten homes and a population of fifty, attracting cattle rustlers, buffalo hunters, gamblers, and businessmen. But, sooner or later, civilization ruins everyone's fun and in 1870, a school was started by Mrs. Margaret

New Quartermaster Storehouse, 1892. Reprinted with the permission of Chris Hale.

Quartermaster Storehouse, the largest stone building in the Fort Clark Guest Ranch, with over 15,000 square feet of storage space, 2005.

Post Bandstand, located in front of the Commanding Officer's quarters, c. 1880s. Reprinted with the permission of William Haenn.

Vertical post and horizontal log cottage, one of the first permanent officers quarters built in 1854, c. 1960s. Reprinted with the permission of William Haenn/Warren Studios, Del Rio, Texas.

One of the many mess halls located at Fort Clark. Attached to the rear of the Infantry Barracks, soldiers would stand in line outside the mess hall and wait their turns.

December 1959. Catered by Rolly Harper, film crew members in a mess hall enjoyed a sumptuous feast including flounder, tartar sauce, New York steak, mashed potatoes and corn.

Powder Magazine and Guardhouse, c. 1887. The small square white building in the center of the photograph is the powder magazine; the fenced building to the left is the Guardhouse. Brackettville and Las Moras Mountain can be seen in the distance. Reprinted with the permission of Chris Hale.

Martin Ballantyne; classes were held in Oscar Brackett's home. At the time, the community was known as Brackett or Brackett City. In 1873, the village even gained a post office, but another Texas town was already known as Brackett. Solution? Just add "ville" to the name. When Capt. R.G. Carter, aide to Col. Ranald Mackenzie, Fourth Cavalry, first gazed upon the village that year, he observed, "Its composition varied somewhat, but there were these inevitable adobe houses, Mexican ranches of 'shacks,' huts, 'jacals' and picket stores… Mexican 'greasers,' half-breeds of every hue and complexion, full-blooded descendants of the African persuasion, low down whites and discharged soldiers, with no visible occupation, composed the population, and at night a fusillade of shots warned us that it was unsafe venturing over after dark on the one crooked, unlighted and wretched street–Le Boulevard de Brackettville." Another officer described it as "the ulcer of [a] garrison, an inevitable fungus growth–profusely plastered with mud, used for whiskey shops, gambling saloons." Most visitors to Brackettville seemed to have agreed with that opinion. The town had been a stop for many of the wagon trains traveling the "lower-road" from Texas to California and Fort Clark was generally the first stop after a bone-jarring, torturous twenty-four-hour trip from San Antone. Period newspaper reporters recalled Brackettville soon mushroomed into a brawling frontier town: "Cattle rustlers and desperados mingled with the wagon train families, buffalo hunters and troops on the streets where every man carried a gun and knew how to use it." An overnight visitor at the Sargent hotel, a local rustic rest stop operated by a Mr. Sheedy, recalled, "We visited the town after supper, and you may imagine our surprise to find ourselves in the liveliest burg in West Texas, where the night life could only be compared to the saloons and gambling places that existed (in) the early days of the gold excitement of California and the Klondike."[11]

The Sargent Hotel. Reprinted with the permission of William Haenn.

Kinney County had been carved out of Bexar County in 1850, two years before Fort Clark was opened as a frontier outpost. (New counties could be established if one hundred free male inhabitants living in the area containing at least nine hundred square miles petitioned the government. To assure that residents would be able to travel to the county seat and return home in one day, the counties were to be roughly thirty miles across with the county seat within five miles of the center.) The first county-owned courthouse was built in Brackettville in 1878/79 and local commissioners desired to build a larger structure in 1891. "Expansion of the army post at Fort Clark led to the subsequent growth of the town. This growth was not all peaceful (as) Brackettville held many time more saloons than churches. The courthouse served a significant role in reversing this situation. The law and lawmen were kept busy keeping the peace. The level of peacekeeping activity made it necessary for the county to expand current quarters or build a new courthouse." The courthouse served that purpose for thirty-two years until 1911 when it became headquarters for the Las Moras Masonic Lodge, which had been chartered in 1876. (This structure later housed the post office from 1918-1983. In 1911, a new courthouse was built in the Beaux Arts Classical style.) Limestone was the prevailing building material in Brackettville: "Everywhere in the hills, quarries of limestone for building purposes crop out conveniently, making rock houses almost as cheap as lumber and practically indestructible." As a result, the 1870s and '80s saw the construction of dozens of both limestone and wooden buildings including the Ann Ross Home (1870s–namesake of Ann Street), Barber Shop, Boot maker, Harness Shop (1870s), Kornrump Saloon (1870s) and Brackett School House built on the grounds of the Brackett Independent School District in September 1883. This was followed by the Jail (1884), Roach/Peterson Building (1885), Veltmann Building (1885), Bucket of Blood Saloon (1885) and the Partrick Hotel (1885).[12]

An infrequent snowstorm in Brackettville, 1897. The Blacksmith shop and Livery stables face Ann Street. Reprinted with the permission of Zack Davis.

The N.P. Petersen & Co. Building, c. 1900. Reprinted with the permission of Zack Davis.

The Joseph Veltman & Son Store, located on Ann Street, c. 1890s. Reprinted with the permission of Zack Davis.

Advertising "Paul Jones Pure Rye," this saloon in the James Cornell Building, on the corner of Post Street (now Ann Street) and Spring Street, would later become McCabe's Drug Store, c. 1896. Conveniently, the Commissioner's Court met on the second floor. Reprinted with the permission of Zack Davis.

As the fort expanded, so did the town's prosperity and at one time, Brackettville was the most important town in this vast section of unmapped Southwest Texas. The area's few ranchers would ride fifty to a hundred miles just to get to town for an evening's entertainment or a chat with other ranchers, or maybe to pick up enough supplies to last another six months before the next trip to town. When troops had been stationed at the local army base, things were hopping. In an article for the *New York Herald Tribune*, an enlisted man stationed at the fort in 1889 painted the town as a raucous frontier town: "Adjacent to Fort Clark, across a narrow stream dignified by the name of Las

The largest general merchandise store in Kinney County, Roach & Co. was continued by N.P. Petersen upon the death of Mr. Roach. Reprinted with the permission of Zack Davis.

Moras River, was Brackettville, a nondescript frontier town, ten miles from the railroad. County seat of Kinney County and about the worst place on the map. Everything ever pictured in the 'movies' of the wildest kind was there, and lots more. The population was some 500, mostly Mexicans. Saloons were on every corner and plenty in between. Dance halls, brothels–let your imagination run riot and you may approximate what this town was in those hectic days… there were several kinds of dances indulged in that are not seen on stage or ballroom floor. There was cheap liquor, cards, all kinds of gambling, women and no legal restraint." With an abundance of saloons, law enforcement officials had their hands full. It's been said that the army placed metal cages around town and in back alleys to hold the rowdy troops–keeping them off the streets until they were taken back to the fort to serve their time. Jasper Ewing Brady wrote in the *New York Herald Tribune*, "The morning after payday there were 110 men confined in the guard house or under arrest charged with every crime in the calendar, from drunkenness to A.W.O.L. up to and including attempted murder."[13]

Ann Street looking north toward Las Moras Mountain, c. 1890s. The post office is on the left. Immediately across the street is boot maker A. Studer. Further down the street is the county jail. Reprinted with the permission of Zack Davis.

The Brackett News office, once again on the east side of Ann Street, c. 1910. Reprinted with the permission of Zack Davis.

Erected in the early 1870s, this Ann Street building served as the first post office and Kinney County Courthouse, c. 1891. Reprinted with the permission of Zack Davis.

Stone buildings housed residences and businesses; with their sharp, angular architecture, these structures attest to the town's past: simple, solid, sturdy. The town was constructed in the shape of an irregular "T." Coming to Brackettville from the east, one entered town at the top of the "T" (Spring Street), the handle of the letter, or the post (Ann Street, aka West 3rd, Ranch to Market 574), ran toward the right. After traveling a bit, you would come to a square, the center of which had a courthouse. In 1882, the Galveston, Harrisburg and San Antonio Railway had originally planned to route its westward track through Brackettville but instead followed an alternate path ten miles south of the community, through Spofford. Combined with devastating floods in 1880 and 1899, many local residents either moved to higher elevations or completely out of town. (Floods would continue to ravage Brackettville in 1932, 1948, 1949, 1951, 1955 and 1957. The most severe flood occurred on June 17, 1958, and encompassed 966 acres of agricultural land and 35 city blocks.) The town's population would ebb and flow, ever-changing due to internal and external influences and the expansion or reduction of the army post, which naturally affected the town's subsequent growth or decline. In 1884, Brackettville had an estimated population of fourteen hundred. By 1896, two years before the Spanish-American War, only one thousand remained and during the Mexican Revolution of 1914-1917, just eight hundred were left. With Pancho Villa raiding both sides of the Rio Grande, attacking settlements and plundering ranches, it's no wonder the community felt in danger and accordingly lost some of its residents. (On March 9, 1916, between five hundred and one thousand Mexican revolutionaries attacked Columbus, New Mexico, which was garrisoned by a detachment of the U.S. Thirteenth Cavalry. Eighteen soldiers and citizens were killed and the town burned. President Woodrow Wilson responded by sending ten thousand troops under the command of Brig. General John J. Pershing to find and capture Villa. Though they spent eleven months unsuccessfully chasing the bandit, they did succeed in destabilizing Villa's forces. In January 1917, under intense pressure from the Mexican government and with an impending European declaration of war, Pershing's forces were withdrawn.)

Prior to Villa's raid, there had been talk that Fort Clark would be closed. Now, such talk was out of the question, and once the 1918 armistice was signed and hostilities ended, the post began a rapid period of expansion, as did Brackettville. Over the next twenty years the fort would grow to include fourteen sets of officers' quarters, six N.C.O. quarters, ten two-story barracks, five administration buildings, ten stables, five storehouses, a service club, barbershop, post exchange, commissary, theater and a restaurant. In 1931, two barracks were re-built on the foundations of those built in 1873 and joined to the single-story 1885 rear buildings to create a "U" shape. By the following year two more barracks were constructed.[14]

By 1927, Brackettville's population increased 150 percent to almost two thousand residents, 75 percent of whom were of Mexican or Seminole-Negro ancestry. Sixteen years later, at the height of the United States' involvement in the latest war to end all wars, it was almost four thousand!

By the early 1940s, with over ten thousand soldiers stationed there, Fort Clark was definitely influencing Brackettville's economy. Soldiers on leave would come to town, spend their time and well-earned dollars at the movie theater or perhaps take their girlfriends to a dance or restaurant. Taverns were available if someone wanted something stronger than soda-pop, and they could always hang out on the corner at McCabe's Drug Store. While Fort Clark's history had always been

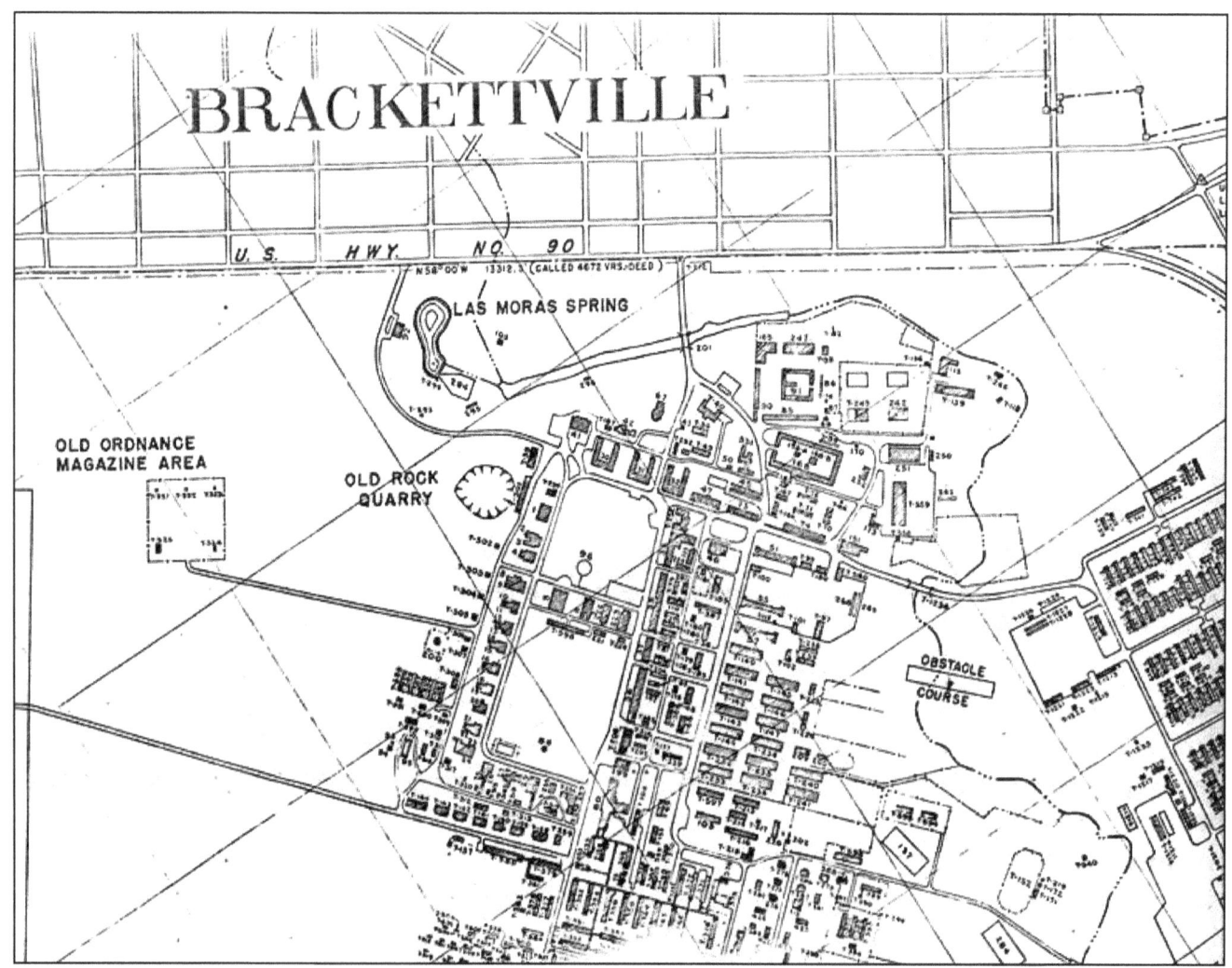

Map of Fort Clark, 1944. Reprinted with the permission of William Haenn/Friends of the Fort Clark Historic District.

one of support to mounted operations, the mechanization of the horse cavalry during the early 1940s, however, spelled its demise. The fort was eventually closed in June 1944 although official deactivation did not occur until 1946. While German POW's previously barracked there were used to dismantle buildings, all remaining troops and other non-military personnel were transferred to Fort Hood in San Antonio. Consequently, the number of residents in Brackettville decreased from a high point of four thousand eight hundred, to a mere twelve hundred, and as a result, the local economy was severely depressed. Virginia Shahan called it devastating. "The government offered to sell Fort Clark to the community for $1 but the town turned it down," she said. "That's when Happy decided to run for mayor." (The fort was sold a year later to the Texas Railway Equipment Co., a subsidiary of Brown and Root, which purchased it in October 1946 for the sum of $411,250. They removed over $4 million worth of temporary buildings, electrical equipment and other items of value, proceeded to sell the lumber and fixtures from the post-World War II period, renovated

Clark, 1947. This photograph shows what Fort Clark looked like immediately after it was closed. The main gate is at the bottom left, six white-roofed mess halls in parallel rows are seen behind three infantry barracks, and the officer's quarters are visible on the right side of the quadrangle, with the Post Theater, Chapel and Post Headquarters on a street bisecting the parade grounds. Reprinted with the permission of William Haenn/Warren Studio, Del Rio, Texas.

and saved many of the buildings, and in the early 1950s, turned it into the Fort Clark Guest Ranch. At the time of the construction of Alamo Village, the ranch was owned and operated by the Driskill Hotel Co.)[15]

After the base was decommissioned, however, the town faced its future alone and the city council was tasked with assuring it even had a future. The mayor certainly wasn't doing a real great job; in 1943, the town had three thousand five hundred residents but by the mid-50s, that number

---

FAMOUS RESIDENTS OF FORT CLARK

Many infantry and cavalry units, including the famous Ninth and Tenth Horse Cavalry–the Black "Buffalo Soldiers"–were stationed at the fort, as were the First Infantry and Mounted Rifles, six companies of Texas Rangers, one company of the First Artillery, the U.S. Third Infantry, the Second Regiment of the Texas Mounted Rifles, the Fourth and Tenth U.S. Cavalry, and the Twenty-fourth and Twenty-fifth U.S. Infantry Regiments, and the Seminole-Negro Indian Scouts to name a few. (The Scouts were originally drawn from five hundred Seminoles of mixed Indian and black ancestors living in Eagle Pass. Their ancestors were runaway slaves from the plantations of South Carolina and Georgia who had sought refuge in the northern bush lands of Spanish-controlled Florida during the late seventeenth century. They lived among the Seminole Indians but preserved their own culture and traditions. After the Seminole wars in the early 1800s, they were removed to the Indian Territory (currently Oklahoma), but fearing their freedom, they fled to northern Mexico. After the Civil War, and passage of the thirteenth amendment granting freedom to slaves, they returned to the United States. Eventually, some of the now-freed slaves joined the Lipan and Tonkawa Indian Scouts at Fort Duncan. The scouts proved almost superhuman in their ability to track down renegade Indians who foraged against the villagers and ranchers. A Seminole settlement was established on Fort Clark in 1872. The Scouts and their families lived along the course of Las Moras Creek two miles south of the main post garrison. They referred to their village of simple jacal-thatched roofed homes as "the camp." A few descendants of the Scouts remain in the Brackettville area. Located almost three miles due south of the fort on Ranch Road 3348 their graves lie next to those of over one hundred of their ancestors in a cemetery, established in September 1872.) During the Civil War, the post served as a hospital for Confederate troops and in World War II, it became a staging ground for troops being deployed to the Pacific front, as well as a German POW camp. Stationed here were Generals Albert Sidney Johnston, Phillip Sheridan, John Pershing, J.E.B. Stuart, James Longstreet, John Bell Hood, Fitzhugh Lee, George B. McClellan, Ulysses S. Grant, William Tecumseh Sherman, George C. Marshall, Abner Doubleday, George S. Patton Jr. and many others. (Ironically, Charles Edward Travis–the only son of William Barret Travis, commander of the Alamo garrison–was stationed at the post while captain of Company E of the Texas Rangers.)[17]

had declined to less than half. Even the local lumberyard lost 90 percent of its business when the base closed. What was once a thriving community now stood on the brink of becoming a ghost town. There was virtually no farm crop production in the area–this was strictly ranching country. Ninety-three percent of the land in Kinney County was rangeland, only .04 percent was used for crops. Mohair from goats, wool and mutton from sheep, that's big industry. With over 200,000 acres of farmable soil, what they really needed was water. Without rain, the soil was drier than dry. Guajilla, a drought-resistant yielder of forage, shed its yellow leaves. "In this country, guajilla is the last card in the deck," said a local rancher. "When you draw that, you are through." When brush plays out, if you have one hundred head of cattle you have ninety-nine too many. No rain, no moisture. No forage, no cattle. It was as simple as that. If something wasn't done, the town would end up just a gas stop on a lonely highway [16]

(For those who wish to learn more about the history of Fort Clark and Brackettville, I strongly suggest William F. Haenn's "Fort Clark and Brackettville: Land of Heroes." Although only 128 pages in length, it is quite simply a magnificent photographic history of both Fort Clark and Brackettville. Also, the National Register of Historic Places Inventory – Nomination form for Fort Clark, dated September 28, 1979, has an abundance of information and photographs associated with the fort's history. In addition, the Kinney County Historical Commission has published an outstanding series of monographs addressing historical structures in both Fort Clark and Brackettville. All are highly recommended.)

Entrance to the Seminole Indian Scouts Cemetery, located on Ranch Road 3348, three miles south of Fort Clark, 2014.

"Burial Site Of Heroic U.S. Army Men, Families, And Heirs. These Seminoles Came Mainly From Florida About 1850; Lived In Northern Mexico And Texas; Joined Lt. (Later a General) John L. Bullis and Col. Ranald S. Mackenzie In Ridding Texas Of Hostile Indians, 1870s."

Over 100 individuals are buried here, including Medal of Honor recipients Pvt. Adam Paine, Trumpeter Isaac Payne, Scout Pompey Factor and Sgt. John Ward, 2015.

Happy had first tried to convince Hollywood back in 1950 that the area would be a great site for filming movies. His office manager, B.J. Burns, recalled "…he did his homework, took some pictures, hopped on a plane and went to Hollywood." Close friend Bill Moody flew him out on his personal Twin Cessna: "I don't want to take any credit for that. Happy made the pitch. It was all him." After beating down doors for eight days, trying without luck to get an appointment to present his proposal, he was just about ready to call it quits and head home. "He couldn't even get his foot in the door," explained Burns. "I got to thinking," Happy said, "this isn't getting me anywhere. I didn't really know these people. I never had any training in knowing how to approach anybody. All I knew was go at them. And, if you wanted something, just go ask for it. But, I found out that the movie industry was a little different." Finally, in frustration "after getting thrown out of every studio," (on his last scheduled day) he visited Disney Studios. "I'd like to talk to the man in charge of making pictures," said Happy. He admitted he didn't know the man's name, "I just wanted to talk to the man responsible for making pictures." "That's Mr. Disney, but he's not here," said the secretary. "Well, who else can I talk to?" "You can talk to Mr. Lyon, but he's busy." Shahan sat down on the edge of the secretary's desk and laid his cards on the table. "My community is going to die if someone doesn't hear my story," explained Happy. "Before you say no to anything I ask, I just want to sit down and tell you my story," begged Shahan. "I'm getting tired of getting the run-around. I know out here it's a different ballgame from what I'm used to, but I've been number one in everything I've ever been in and (I can't even get anyone to listen to me). How do you get an appointment with these people? You know, being a rancher and a horse trader and a farmer, it's either a deal or it isn't. You buy my potatoes or you don't; you trade horses or you don't." Fortunately, luck was on his side. Walt Disney's executive secretary, Alpha Steinman, was momentarily covering for the front desk receptionist and wanted to hear more. "Are you leveling with me?" she asked. "I sure am," Happy replied. "'Cause if you are," she continued, "I know this guy at Paramount who is planning to do a Western and…" She was sufficiently interested to call her friend and get Happy an appointment with Harry Templeton, an associate to producer Nat Holt. Templeton happened to be a World War II Air Force pilot with the rank of major. Burns continued, "A little later (Shahan) walked into Paramount for his appointment with his hat in hand and said, 'I'm Happy Shahan from Brackettville, Texas. You probably never heard of Happy Shahan or Brackettville.' Harry looked at him and said, 'Well, I don't know about that. Do you know Colonel Hobbs?' Shahan said, 'Yeah, that's my neighbor rancher!' Templeton had been to Brackettville and had hunted at Colonel Hobbs' ranch." Shahan had already been to that studio earlier in the week, but he didn't know who to see: "After thirty minutes when (Templeton) found out I knew Colonel Hobbs, he reached over to his phone, called the colonel, and told him he was sitting there in Hollywood talking with his friend Happy Shahan. That was my first stroke of luck in Hollywood. You have to be at the right place at the right time with the right product. If I'd been five minutes earlier or later (into Disney's office), I would have missed the opportunity to meet with him. I didn't know enough to realize it at the time, but five minutes either way and that first deal might not have worked." As a result, in November/December 1952, Holt produced *Arrowhead*, previously known as *Adobe Wells*, starring Jack Palance, Brian Keith and Charlton Heston, which became the first project that Happy was able to attract to the area. Happy always gave credit to Hobbs for bringing the project to the community. Perhaps he meant if it wasn't for the relationship between Hobbs and Templeton, he would never have been so fortunate. Interestingly, local newspapers said Bob O'Donnell, Interstate Theaters vice-president and general manager, received the credit for persuading Paramount to make the movie in Texas. Regardless as to who was responsible, Hollywood finally came to Brackettville.[18]

"Arrowhead" lobby card starring Charlton Heston, Jack Palance, Katy Jurado and Brian Keith.

In order to drum up additional business for the area, Happy visited the West Coast every three or four months, or maybe once a month for five to ten days, or maybe five times in three years, or whatever, depending upon what day of the week Happy was telling the story. Explained Happy, "People told me that you couldn't sell Brackettville but I say you can sell any place if you sell what it has. I try and get out to Hollywood at least every three months to keep the town's name and its advantages in front of them. I didn't know anything about making movies, but I did know something about putting packages together. I found you can sell those Hollywood people (anything) if you just keep trying." On his own, with no partner, he hustled all around town, touched base with old contacts, made new ones, and generally tried to attract Hollywood to come out once again. He wasn't always successful, but he was persistent: "My wife used to get mad at me the way they'd treat me. I couldn't even get in to see a secretary. But I told her, 'That's all right. Someday, they're going to be calling me.'" Shahan could be pretty stubborn when he wanted something. Having already learned a little more about how to operate, Happy traveled out there so frequently the studio executives picked him up in limousines.[19]

Armed with a briefcase full of photographs of the Brackettville area, taken by Rural Electric Administration manager Tom Hurd, Happy traveled to Hollywood to talk to Herbert Yates, President of Republic Studios, about a movie Yates intended to produce. Although it didn't work out, Yates later called Happy and said, "We're going to do a picture about the Alamo with John Wayne." As Happy recalled, "So we got everybody ready and thought Wayne was coming to make *The Alamo*. It was to be called *Texas and the Alamo*, or something like that." Republic brought builders to construct the sets and Shahan furnished material from Shaker Feed and Lumber, almost $50,000 of lumber, plaster, nails, etc. Happy didn't want any movies filmed on his ranch

Poster for "Last Command," starring Sterling Hayden as Jim Bowie, Anna Maria Alberghetti as Consuelo de Quesada, Richard Carlson as William B. Travis, Arthur Hunnicutt as Davy Crockett, Ernest Borgnine as Mike Radin and J. Carrol Naish as General Antonio Lopez de Santa Anna.

at that time. His job was to build sets and hustle. With movie sets constructed of papier-mâché, "…they didn't spend a whole lot of money on that picture," explained Shahan. "Herb Yates… who had made millions on B-Westerns, didn't want to spend the money Wayne wanted to spend. But Wayne and Mr. Yates got into an argument and they parted company. Wayne owned the title. (He) wouldn't allow Yates to use 'The Alamo' in the title." It was obvious that this wasn't the epic picture that Wayne had planned. Of course, Wayne wasn't too upset about that project as evidenced by his comments; Yates tried to "steal the idea," said Duke. "(He) came up with *The Last Command* (produced in March/April 1955 starring Sterling Hayden, Ernest Borgnine, Arthur Hunnicutt and Anna Maria Alberghetti) which was a quickie. Nuff said." Wayne laughed, "Instead of five thousand Mexican soldiers, Republic had one hundred fifty, spaced eighteen feet apart." Chuck Roberson, stunt double for Wayne, and one of Crockett's Tennesseans in *The Alamo*, summed it up nicely: "I was on the picture (*Last Command*) and it was just like any other quickie Western Yates produced." Local residents got a kick out of telling everyone that a pickup truck could be seen on the horizon when Mexican soldiers charged some mock-up and not-very-authentic Alamo walls. As a result of near-sighted cameramen, the film was exhibited around the world including

Taking a rest on the set of "Last Command." Sterling Hayden, Ben Cooper as Jeb Lacey and John Russell as Lt. Dickinson. Supposedly, the set piece representing the Long Barrack was on wheels so it could be moved out of the way when not needed.

The Main Gate of "Last Command's" the Alamo compound. Note the significant difference in architectural style between "Last Command" and "The Alamo." The set was built on the Louis Hobbs ranch, five miles south of Brackettville on the Spofford road. With Long Barrack, Low Barrack and palisade, the set didn't include the Alamo chapel which eventually was represented via a matte painting.

that vehicle. One London critic editorially wondered how a truck got mixed up in a charge of 1836 troops.[20]

(Interestingly, in her May 7, 1958 column, Louella Parsons wrote that Yul Brynner and Alan Ladd planned to pool their respective production companies to make a film about the Alamo also planned for a 1959 release. Obviously this would have been a continuation of Ladd's portrayal of James Bowie seen in 1952's *The Iron Mistress*.[21])

During the filming of *Last Command*, Happy had a conversation with a stunt man who worked on the set and learned about Wayne's intention to still make a movie about the Alamo. He heard the same thing from actor Ernest Borgnine as well. Happy said he met Borgnine when he went to the set to deliver a telegram that informed the actor he'd been nominated for an Academy Award for *Marty*. During their conversation, Happy asked why Wayne was there and was told Wayne along with screenwriter James Edward Grant had left Republic Studios. Shahan later confirmed the story with his contacts at Republic. All wasn't lost, though. He did obtain Wayne's phone number while on the set. After Wayne and Yates' parting-of-the-ways, Duke had second thoughts

A mockup poster for the Alamo film Herbert Yates intended to make. Based on her appearance in the poster, it seems Gail Russell was intended to play Wayne's love interest.

and indicated he would still be willing to do the film even though he wasn't employed at Republic any longer. Yates waffled about the quality of the script, so Duke said, "Well, just give it back to me—I'll pay you whatever you want." Yates refused. He hired interim scriptwriter Allen Rivkin to polish the script after Warren Duff was unavailable and asked Wayne to reconsider. Duke analyzed the changes, realized the script direction and content was not to his liking and, once again and for the final time, rejected Yates' offer. But Wayne wasn't finished. He contacted his good friend Robert Newman, who worked at Republic. "I tell you what you do," he told Newman. "Tell Yates to give you that story of Jimmy Grant's for a dollar, and I'll give you twenty thousand dollars for it." Sounded reasonable, but Yates wouldn't go for it. As a result, the script Grant worked so long and hard on was still owned by Yates and had been reworked into the movie they now were shooting.[22]

Happy stated he heard Wayne's intended project was going to be filmed in Mexico and, of course, being a Texan, he couldn't swallow that, so in April 1955, Happy called Wayne directly, first speaking to Mary St. John, Wayne's secretary, and eventually to Wayne himself. "I called him Mr. Wayne," stated Happy. "That's the only time I ever called him Mr. Wayne. I said, 'I understand you want to do a picture called *The Alamo*.' Wayne said, 'I'm going to do a picture called *The Alamo*.' I said, 'Where are you going to do it?' He said, 'In Mexico or Panama.' I said, 'You can't do it.' Wayne said, 'I can do it any god damn place I want to.'" Shahan told him, "'Hey, look, you've got problems you don't know you've got.' He was just as hardheaded as I was. I finally said, 'We're not getting anywhere with this. Why don't I just get on a plane and come out there and talk with you about your favorite subject–*The Alamo*?' 'Fine,' he said, so I went out, and we visited, had a good time. He gave me sound reasons for shooting it in Mexico. They were sound reasons for *him*, but they really weren't sound reasons for a picture of that type. We argued and dickered and I went back home. But, I told him the Daughters of the Republic of Texas (DRT) wouldn't stand for that." Duke had published a news release about the possibility of shooting in Mexico and, just as Happy predicted, the DRT reacted exactly as Happy said it would. R. J. (Bob) O'Donnell, who owned a chain of movie theatres, and Jesse Jones, the publisher of the *Houston Chronicle*, both indicated to the DRT that *they* wouldn't support a film about the Alamo if it was made in Mexico and furthermore, wouldn't allow it to be shown in Texas cinemas. "Wayne thought I put (the DRT) up to it, but I didn't," admitted Shahan. "It's just one of those things… He had property down there in Durango, and he had already shot some pictures down there. He just thought he would do *The Alamo* down there. He found out, though, that the politics would eat him up down there. At one point when he'd gotten really serious about building the sets in Mexico, he'd had a million 'dobes made down there for use in the sets. Then he found out they had made them into little houses. The Mexican there had sold them all. They used 'em more than he did. So things just began to snowball on him. I had a lot of respect for Wayne, but we didn't mind arguing. Wayne was like I am, I guess—headstrong and used to getting his own way." Although Happy didn't coordinate the DRT response, he did start a letter-writing campaign called "Make the Alamo in Texas" to try and persuade Wayne to make the right choice. In later years, Shahan told his office manager B.J. that, in fact, *he* had spearheaded the campaign.[23]

An outraged, furious Wayne called Happy, accused him of underhanded behavior and demanded to know why he was behind this vicious behavior, but Happy pleaded ignorance. After tempers cooled and Happy had convinced Wayne that he wasn't really the culprit, they got down to seriously discussing the opportunity. Asked Happy, "Why don't you at least come down to check out the location before you reject the suggestion?" Wayne realized that filming the project in Texas, as Shahan suggested, would also help him obtain the necessary financing. Still, the costs would be greater than they would have been otherwise had filming taken place outside the U.S. Attracting a major film such as *The Alamo* would be a giant shot in the arm for Brackettville.[24]

As early as 1947, Wayne and James Grant had visited San Antonio, then hired a research group to pull together all the information it could find on the Alamo in preparation for an eventual movie. In March of the following year, Wayne, director John Ford, Ward Bond, Merian C. Cooper and D. L. (Tex) Hill visited San Antonio while searching for locations for the production of *Three Godfathers*, which would star Wayne, Pedro Armendáriz and Harry Carey Jr. At that time, Wayne spoke about a contemplated motion picture about the siege of the Alamo. Ford said that filming of the battle was being considered with Wayne playing the role of Davy Crockett. The film would be confined to the actual battle along with events leading up to it. Ford said, "It may be a year before we start shooting scenes of the Alamo picture." After completing the film *Jet Pilot* in 1950, Wayne took his wife, Chata, down to Central America where he made a tentative search for possible locations for the projected film. By 1951, it was apparent that Wayne was getting more and more serious about bringing *The Alamo* to fruition, as an announcement was made about mid-year that he intended to make the film in Mexico City. It was actually Durango, not Mexico City, but that didn't make any difference. As might be expected, the proposed location didn't sit too well with Texas. Hedda Hopper summed it up nicely in her newspaper column when she said, "Texas is ready to start a shootin' war since they learned that John Wayne will make *The Alamo* in Mexico City. (Perhaps they were referring to Churubusco Studios. Interestingly, Alfred Ybarra, who would be art director on *The Alamo*, was one of the original architects of this facility.) If he does, two important Texans– Jesse Jones and Bob O'Donnell may take steps to boycott the film. My guess is that Duke Wayne will proceed as planned, hoping the publicity will increase the value of the picture; but I'd sure rather have Texas fer me than agin me." On June 21, 1951, Bob O'Donnell wrote a letter to Herbert Yates expressing his concern about the mounting negative reaction Wayne was receiving after announcing he planned to film the project in Mexico: "To make the story of the Alamo in Mexico City would be disastrous, in my opinion, and would be like making the story of Bunker Hill or the Liberty Bell in Philadelphia or any of our patriotic stories in a foreign country… I definitely know

"John Wayne, movie star, and John Ford, a film producer, spent several hours at the Alamo and museum… gathering historical data." Reprinted with the permission of the Institute of Texan Cultures.

John Wayne, producer Merian C. Cooper and actor Ward Bond examine a long rifle used in defense of the Alamo.

that it would damn it immeasurably in Texas." O'Donnell also asked that if Wayne was considering it, was there anything that O'Donnell and Yates could do to change his mind?[25]

Because of the fallout from the previous publicity, Wayne appeared to clarify his position in October. Touring Texas with Greer Garson, Dan Dailey, Jeff Chandler, Keenan Wynn, Wendell Cory, Chill Wills, director King Vidor, producer Jesse L. Lasky, Sr., and six starlets called "The Golden Circle of Stars"–the tour was to acquaint the public with the motion picture industry, celebrate the fiftieth anniversary of motion pictures, and, promote "Movie time U.S.A."–Wayne stated that shooting the film in San Antonio would cost him "a million dollars more" than if he did so in California or Mexico. Wayne did indicate "We would like to use the interior of the Alamo for some of the shots. We will use the chapel if they will let us." Wayne wanted to shoot "a couple of scenes in the Alamo" for background material. He felt that although the present appearance of the Alamo didn't lend itself to the period of 1836, he believed that some arrangement could be made to film the chapel scenes. During this conversation, Ken McClure, a former movie consultant who was engaged by the San Antonio local municipal advertising commission, challenged Wayne's commitment to the project. "You wouldn't shoot the battle of Bunker Hill in Mexico, would you?" he asked. Wayne responded, "They didn't shoot *Gone With The Wind* in the south." Wayne further explained that he had already invested several years in the planning of this project and since it was going to be his first big picture, he's "not going to make a cheap job of it." McClure had signed a $5,000 contract with the commission in an attempt to negotiate with the producers of the film to have it shot locally. Although convinced that the city had very little hope in having the decision reversed, San Antonio Mayor Jack White indicated that a last-ditch effort would be made. It soon appeared that Republic never really had any intention of filming the project in San Antonio. On Wednesday, October 10, the city had received a letter from William Saal, who was Yates' executive assistant. Saal wrote, "If we had known that we weren't going to start *The Alamo* until spring, we would have made a motion picture named *The Golden Herd* which was written by a Texan man and had its locale near San Antonio. No doubt we will make this picture in your territory." Saal also reminded the mayor that snaring a major motion picture requires many months of groundwork but noted the city was well on the road to having pictures made in the area. In any case, they were unsuccessful. Wayne explained his reasoning: "I went to the Mexican government in 1951 and presented my script to the Censor Board, then under the Cabinet Seat of Mr. Martinez, who found no fault with our script, after inviting us to meet with top Mexican representatives chosen for their historical knowledge. I went to the Sindicados in Mexico and gained their permission to make it in Mexico, if I wished. At that time financial problems postponed the making of the motion picture."[26]

In July 1952, Wayne made a trip to Peru, accompanied by long-time friend and Wayne-Fellows production assistant Ernie Saftig to look at potential locations and possible investments, as well as to take a vacation. RKO studios and Panagra (Pan-American Grace Airways) arranged the trip and Wayne was also to make goodwill visits to distributors of American Films in South America. While there, although not finding anything that suited his requirements, he was introduced to Pilar Weldy (Pallete), a young Peruvian actress appearing in the movie *Green Hell*. She would eventually become his third wife. As Wayne also had a number of financial investments in Panama at that time, including a partnership in a shrimp business with the former ambassador to Great Britain, Robert Tito Arias, it seemed that a suitable location might be found there. He was convinced that the awesome truth of this courageous, unequaled battle for liberty could only be told by duplicating exactly the physical circumstances of the battle as they occurred. With Wayne's numerous connections, he scouted several locations and discovered one in Latin America that appeared acceptable. The landscaping, scenery and vegetation were similar in appearance to 1836 San Antonio. Accessible via an old abandoned airfield and with reasonable local labor costs, filming south of the border would be a significant cost savings compared to filming it in the U.S. The site also had the necessary accommodations for the sizeable cast and crew. As he said, "I had found a location in (western) Panama… a really perfect setting… that looked exactly like San Antonio back then… There was a perfect area just outside of Panama City… Panama was having a depression right then that would have made the whole operation cheaper. Also, there was a two-mile airstrip nearby that the Americans had built, so transport would have been easy." Wayne discovered it during one of his trips down the Pacific coast with John Ford. Eventually, however, that project failed to materialize. It *may* have been due to rumors of a pending Panamanian revolution or perhaps Arias' tenuous relationship with the new President Ernesto de la Guardia.[27]

John Wayne and his beautiful wife Pilar arrive at the London premiere of "The Alamo," Charing Cross Road, October 27, 1960.

As a result, early in 1952, Wayne started pre-production in Durango but was forced to abandon the work that was already done on the set when friends in the Mexican government told him that some officials might impede the project. Mexican President Aleman, a friend of Wayne, indicated that personally he wouldn't have an objection with the movie being filmed in Mexico, but "Mexico and the Alamo are sore points. The press will slaughter you." Over one million adobe bricks to be used in the construction of the project also disappeared and found their way into the construction of local housing. After a month of extensive preparation, Wayne was forced to abandon the project. In addition, once he left Republic Studios and Herb Yates, his financing was jeopardized as Yates apparently pushed the impression to Wayne's Texan backers that the film would be made locally. Wayne had received financial commitments predicated upon Republic's involvement in production and distribution. Upon his departure from Republic he was forced to renegotiate with his backers and they insisted that the film be made in Texas. Happy's reasoning, sense of logic, and persistence (over two years of negotiations) convinced Wayne to explore the opportunities in Southern Texas. Of course, Happy also stated that buying Wayne the best Stetson that he could find in San Antonio probably didn't hurt either.[28]

So, in June 1957, Wayne sent Nate Edwards to Brackettville to check out the area and see if it would be suitable for filming purposes. Happy, delighted that someone was actually coming to follow up on his constant pestering, offered to chauffeur Nate around personally. Edwards also brought his wife and soon he and Happy settled into a routine. Each morning, Nate would leave his wife at Fort Clark and Happy would pick him up in a ranch truck, having driven eight miles into town from his Shahan-Angus ranch. Then over the course of a single week, they would spend the rest of each day driving all over the four-county area, looking at potential sites only to return each evening without finding a suitable location. Housing, scenery, climate, local resources, manpower, and accessibility were all critical requirements in the decision-making process. Wayne wanted a location that most resembled the terrain where the actual battle had been fought. They visited river sites on the Nueces River north of Uvalde and on the West Nueces twenty miles north of Brackettville. They also looked at the Davis ranch north of Shahan's where Wayne eventually filmed a scene where the Mexican army crossed a river in front of two large rock bluffs. No doubt they visited the Louis Hobbs ranch and viewed the remains of the *Last Command* Alamo set. (The ranch was located about five miles south of Brackettville. The set's $50,000 pre-fab walls were manufactured in six-foot sections at an abandoned fire station at Fort Clark. Made of wood, chicken-wire and plaster (all supplied by Shahan's Shaker Feed and Lumber), the hollow structures were built to simulate mortared limestone. However, the compound only consisted of two walls (the South Wall and about 150 feet of the West Wall), a false front representing the southernmost end of the Long Barrack complete with "a peculiar tower," a low wall connecting the Long Barrack section to the Low Barrack, and a twelve-foot-high palisade with cannon port. Rather than include the chapel, a part of the façade of the chapel and its ruined interiors were mere painted backdrops. The upper half of the chapel is a poorly executed matte painting. In addition to the matte painting, a part of the facade was "constructed" later on the soundstage. This was the doorway entrance piece immediately framing the shot of the interior "painted backdrop." Conspicuously absent were both the chapel and the village of San Antonio. Each was provided, however, through matte paintings.) They even visited Bill Moody's Leona ranch as several scenes were eventually filmed there including Crockett and his Tennesseans approaching the hill overlooking San Antonio, and Santa Anna's army on the march over hill and dale. But nothing appeared to meet the requirements.[29]

East Pinto Creek looking downstream from behind Alamo Village. Reprinted with the permission of Richard Curilla/ Alamo Village.

"I didn't even bring him to the (Shahan) ranch," explained Happy. "I lived in town. I didn't even want him on the ranch. I

East Pinto Creek on the southeast corner of the Shahan ranch. Alamo Village Archives 2462-4.

Las Moras Mountain, between the Shahan ranch and Brackettville. The photograph may have been taken from a point southeast of the village. Alamo Village Archives 2362-03B.

The road to Ten-Mile looking southwest towards the Alamo set and village. The airstrip is along the whole ridge running from left to right. The very right edge of the picture is approximately where the faux Alamo top is located. Alamo Village Archives 2462-03C.

East Pinto Creek directly behind Alamo Village. Normally a dry arroyo, it only has running water when the canyons to the northeast flood. Reprinted with the permission of Kristi Hale.

Standing on the slope of "Parson's Hill," a lone individual gazes upon the site where "The Alamo" set will be constructed. The village of San Antonio was built in front of the trees that line East Pinto Creek in the mid-distance. The future Alamo compound would be built off the right side of the photo. "Parson's Hill" is located behind the Alamo and is the spot from which Crockett, Smitty, Parson and the Tennesseans first view San Antonio. Alamo Village Archives.

never hustled a picture for our (place) 'cause I didn't want to make (any) pictures (there). My job was building sets for them. Ranching was my business, by then I'd become successful." That was sufficient for him.[30]

At around 4:30 p.m. on the last day of Edwards' visit, Happy decided to call it a day. They were hot, tired, and hadn't found anything suitable yet, and there really wasn't anything left to show. Happy mentioned that he wanted to stop at his ranch to cut out a few head of cattle and Nate asked if he could come along as he had been born and raised on a ranch in El Paso but left when he was twenty-one to work in the movie industry. Later that evening, the two men planned to cross the border at Acuña and have dinner with their wives. No doubt discussing where to eat, they drove past a "bull trap" pasture on their way to "Ten-Mile," a loading pen and house located about three miles from Shahan's office. Nate's head rapidly turned left and right as they drove over the pasture. He challenged Happy as to why he hadn't suggested this location. "You know, this is the prettiest spot there is," said Edwards. Happy explained that he didn't think Nate would be interested–he wanted to show him the whole area. Using his hands as a viewfinder, Edwards exclaimed, "I think this is what we're looking for." He then got out of the truck and, surrounded by mesquite, prickly pear cactus, blackbrush, postoak, and guillo chaparral, took some photos. Nate was going to leave the next day but canceled his flight and came back to take another look at the site. Impressed, he shot one hundred or so more photos in a 360 degree panoramic view and then returned to

California. There, he enlarged the photographs, displayed them in a ten-foot circle in Wayne's office, and presented them to his boss. Wayne liked what he saw.[31]

In an interview Tully Shahan gave to Dr. Larry Butler for the program *Out on the Land*, he describes a slightly different version of how the spot was picked out: "There's a story about them finding this location. There's a road that goes from headquarters to Ten-Mile. It's called Ten-Mile because it's ten miles from Brackettville. The location man was here and he was here for three or four days and Dad had taken him all over the county to different ranches; they were trying to find a location. He asked this location manager, 'I gotta go to Ten-Mile for a shearing over there. They're shearing sheep. I gotta go over there to check the shearing and see what they need. Do you wanta go with me?' So on the way, while they drive through (the ranch), this man says, 'Hold it! Hold it. Stop right here. Let me get out and you pick me up when you come back.' And so this guy walks around, Dad's gone I don't know how long. But he comes back and this guy says, 'Happy, we're going to do it right here.' And that's how this location was discovered. I remember the night, we were living in town and Mother had just cooked steaks. We had just cooked steaks. Back then you broiled all your steaks but we killed our own beef. After supper (Nate Edwards) called California on the phone. I remember him walking out of that door saying, 'We're filming it in Texas!' And that was a joyous occasion in our house that night."[32]

Shortly after Edwards' visit, Shahan resigned as mayor of Brackettville: "I just got tired of local politics. I wrote a letter and resigned as mayor. And it wasn't anything anybody was doing to me, I just got tired of all the old lady friends of mine, the grandmas calling for a load of caliche in their front driveway, that sort of thing, and that wasn't even my department. It was the pressure of trying to satisfy everybody, I got tired. So, I resigned." On July 2, he grabbed his wife and kids, got in his car, drove to Lake Louise, Alberta, Canada, and took an extended vacation which he did every summer.[33]

Two months went by with no indication as to what the decision would be so, in the latter part of August, Happy drove to Los Angeles on his way back home and stopped in to see Wayne. Shahan hadn't heard anything after Edwards' visit in June and wondered what Wayne was going to do. No surprise there; that summer Wayne was in London and Rome completing the final edit on *Legend of the Lost*. Happy may have received a call from Mary St. John, Wayne's secretary, indicating that Duke wanted to see him. Nevertheless, he sent Virginia and the children back to Brackettville and then headed to Los Angeles. When he walked into Wayne's Batjac office Happy saw the enlarged photos of the site, so he and Duke started discussing what would be required. And Wayne couldn't have been more agreeable. Happy listened with great interest: Wayne wanted to make the movie, Happy wanted it made. What more could you ask for? When Herb Yates continued to let people believe Wayne's project would be filmed in Texas, not Mexico as initially planned, Duke had no choice but to change direction, even though it would cost significantly more. And Happy's ranch fit the bill: hill, valleys, and rolling plains, scenic Pinto Mountain as a background. Streams and creeks. A decommissioned army base to serve as base camp. The Mexican border just a half-hour away, close enough to attract the numerous extras needed. All that was left was for Wayne to give the location his blessing. According to Shahan, "Wayne said he liked it. 'I like it. I'd like to do it there. But I don't know for sure what we're going to do. I've already got a million 'dobes made in Mexico and I'll make it down there.'" After additional discussion, Shahan left the office.[34]

By early September Wayne had made up his mind. He called Shahan and said he was flying to Brackettville to look at the site himself. When asked when, Duke said, "Tomorrow!" Along with son Michael, he arrived with art director Al Ybarra and all agreed the location met every expectation. Happy was at a neighbor's ranch at the time and although Duke seemed pleased with the site he was apprehensive when it came to set construction. Even though he and Shahan had had numerous meetings and discussions over the past two years, Wayne was still skeptical as to how the set actually would be built. "There was a doubt in their mind because, who was I?" said Shahan. "They just knew me to argue and maybe go have dinner with." Shahan told Wayne, "Fourteen years you've been trying to make this picture. All I want is an architect, your art director, and that's all. I can do the rest." Rather than use Hollywood crews, Happy insisted that his construction firm's workmen could build a permanent set, rather than the temporary ones traditionally used in the industry, which made perfect sense because otherwise Hollywood union costs would be astronomical! As Happy pointed out, "There's no telling what it would have cost him." Wayne still wanted reassurance it was possible, so Happy sent a man to town to bring his construction foreman out to the ranch. As this supervisor stepped from the pickup truck, Wayne just shook his head with an expression that said, "You gotta be kidding!" The colorful, five-foot-two-inch, forty-year-old World War II veteran, Jose "Chato" Alvarez Hernandez, Jr. wasn't an imposing figure. But he knew his trade. Chato, who had dropped out of school at an early age to help his grandfather support the family, had been in the construction business for quite some time and Happy initially had contacted him several years earlier in Eagle Pass where he was a general contractor. Skilled in carpentry, bricklaying, roofing, framing, and foundations, Hernandez had honed his proficiency through the Works Progress Administration

Master craftsman Jose "Chato" Alvarez Hernandez, Jr.

(WPA) program started by Franklin D. Roosevelt. According to daughter Margarita, "My dad didn't have a lot of school. He dropped out to help my grandfather support the family. All my dad learned about the construction business he learned on his own. He had a lot of books and loved to learn about new tools." Chato also was well known in the local area for his carpentry skills as he had already completed work for such local ranches as the Anacacho, Hildalgo, Leona, Bader, Conley and Frerich. Chato had also previously worked on the *Last Command* set and completely remodeled Happy's ranch house as well. Shahan recalled, "He (Chato) was about five-foot-three, about that wide, didn't finish the third grade in Mexico, could speak English very little but understood English, understood anything you said." Of course, that didn't really cut any weight with Wayne–he had to assure himself that he was going to get what he expected.[35]

So Duke decided to have Chato questioned… for almost two hours! He asked about his background, construction experience, prior jobs–anything that would give him a sense of the individual and his skill. Hernandez was asked to identify various architectural drafting symbols that Ybarra drew: concealed wiring or center lines, property lines, compacted earth fill, framing lumber,

Laborers were hired from the surrounding areas in addition to Mexico. In many cases, it was a family affair. Left to right: Chato Hernandez, a friend from Eagle Pass, Victor Jimmez and Severiano Hernandez.

electrical lines, etc., etc., etc. Finally satisfied with Chato's background, experience and knowledge, Wayne asked one last question: "Chato, do you really think that you can build me the Alamo?" Chato paused for a moment, looked up directly into Wayne's eyes, smiled and said, "Do you think you can make a picture?" Well, Wayne laughed so hard he had to sit on the ground. Laughed until tears came to his eyes. "That good enough for me!" he said. Hernandez initially commuted the one hundred miles each day to assist in the construction of the set. When that became too great a strain, the family moved to Brackettville and rented a house. Working on the set became a family affair as Chato, his brothers Sostenes and Severiano ("Cheve"), cousin Victor Jimenez and nephews Manuel Roman and Jose Luis Rodriguez were all involved in one way or another. Wayne must have thought very highly of Chato's work, for after the picture wrapped, Duke approached him and asked several times if he and his family would move to California and work for Wayne. Chato had to turn down the request because his wife didn't want to leave Brackettville.[36]

"(Wayne) would have done his picture somewhere, sometime," recalled Happy, "but what caused him to do his picture here was my saying that all I needed was his art director, and I would see to the construction of his sets. I said, 'We'll do the picture the way you want it done. It's your picture.' In other words, I would see to it that he got his sets the way he wanted them for the picture. All I needed was a blueprint. I owned a building company here that could supply everything he required in the way of sets for the picture. All I needed from him was a 'Yes.'"[37]

Happy said, "I made a deal with John Wayne in 1957 in September and started building the next day. We argued until September 1957… We argued a lot of places, but we always argued. It took me two years to convince Duke that I could do what I said I could do." Wayne was to fly out to the site about once a month to check on the progress. Bill Moody often ferried Wayne back and forth to wherever Duke needed to go: On August 9, 1958, Moody flew Patrick, Michael and Duke to the Las Vegas Riviera to see Red Skelton's show—Wayne was introduced from the audience and stood up to an ovation. And three days before filming began in 1959, Wayne had an ear infection so Moody took him to a doctor in San Antonio. They rode an elevator up to the office and when they came back down, the lobby was filled with fans. Moody was even asked for autographs. When he replied, "I'm not an actor," Wayne merely leaned over and said, "Just sign it, Billy boy."[38]

Obviously, the availability of water was going to be a huge issue: water for livestock, water for irrigation, water for domestic use for production groups and technicians, and water to manufacture adobe blocks. Wayne wanted to know where all this water would come from. Happy knew where it was to be found but Wayne didn't believe him. According to Shahan, their conversation went as follows:

Wayne: "Where's your water?"
Shahan: "Underground."
Wayne: "How do you know there's water underground?"
Shahan: "Look, I said there's water underground."
Wayne: "You're not God!"
Shahan: "Hey, I didn't say that, but I know there's water underground because I know the formations here."[39]

Wayne suggested they drill for water on the crest of a gentle nearby hill. "It looked like the worst place on my ranch to drill for water," said Shahan. "Still, we humored John. And the other day, we got a regular water gusher. Thousands of gallons! The well driller said we tapped an underground lake at 135 feet. Gosh! If I could have just had John Wayne here during the drought telling me where to drill for water!" Hoping to get fifty gallons per minute, the well tested three hundred fifty gallons per minute for three hours without noticeably lowering the level of the water. To hype the publicity, Happy later exaggerated that amount to "one thousand gallons per minute!" A large concrete twenty-five thousand two hundred-gallon reservoir was built at a cost of $5,000 for storage, with an electric pump to keep the water flowing. Open the floodgates and Pinto Creek became the San Antonio River! Later, Happy again substantially changed the story–Wayne planned to put the well inside the Alamo compound, which wouldn't work since noise from the generators would be heard on the film's soundtrack. Happy said it would be better on top of a nearby hill, but Wayne scoffed at the idea because it would mean drilling farther to get to the water. Happy told him no, it didn't. He then brought Charles Dolstrum out from Fort Clark, who arrived complete with a willow wand and started witching. Happy drew a ten-foot circle and told Charlie water could be found in there somewhere. Immediately, the wand went down. "Gimme that!" Wayne said, grabbing the stick. He also felt the tug. "Fine, Shahan. We'll drill it here," relented Wayne, "but if there's no water, you'll pay for the well." They did and there was. The next day, according to Happy, there was a headline in a Dallas newspaper: "John Wayne Witches for Water on Shahan Ranch." Happy said he knew Wayne needed publicity and he got it for him. Wayne had a slightly different recollection of the event. When he returned to San Antonio, Duke told local restaurateur Big John Hamilton that *he* discovered the well. Apparently Wayne was one of those few lucky souls who possess "hidden powers." Armed with a "fresh Y-shaped willow branch," he wandered over Shahan's ranch, looking for a spot to drill a well. With the bottom of the "Y" pointed downward, the branch suddenly "came alive," beginning to twist away from him until it pointed directly at the ground. Shahan started digging a well at that location. Either way, water was discovered.[40]

"It served two purposes," related Ybarra, "'cause we piped water in from the church itself down to the village, in the event of fire. And we put a five-hundred-gallon tank down in the soil with pumps on it to provide water… to prevent fire. We kept fire hoses and everything there. Up in the main tank, it served a dual purpose 'cause we had five hundred to six hundred horses up there. We had two dump trucks going constantly to and from the corrals. 'Cause five or six hundred horses, they eat a lot of hay! They make a mess!" A second well was located in the village in addition to Ybarra's five-hundred-gallon tank. Through a three-inch line, it fed three fire hydrant access points strategically located around the village, covered by three-foot by three-foot iron plate trapdoors.[41]

"Regarding a spot for the village in relation to the Alamo church/mission itself: The distance between the village and the Alamo church is approximately a quarter of a mile downhill," Ybarra explained. "In order to determine how big I wanted the village, I had a man go down into the area and I would sit from the position of the Alamo and motion to him. 'Left' and he would stop and wave a flag. Then I'd say, 'Right about a quarter of a mile,' and he'd mark it there. We put two telephone poles; that was the extent of the village proper." Ybarra then shot two wide-angle photos of the terrain. The first was of the countryside as it looked from the viewpoint of the town of San Antonio. Then, four hundred yards away, he placed a marker for the site of the Alamo. From there he took a second photo looking back at the site of San Antonio where the first marker had been placed. On those two photos, he painted complete perspective drawings of the fort and town as they would look when construction was completed.[42]

Once Wayne approved the drawings, construction began in October 1957 and was to take almost twenty-three months before the set was finally completed and ready for filming. However, during preliminary investigation and research, one major problem popped up several times. To assure historical accuracy, Wayne absolutely insisted on the use of adobe bricks in construction of the various structures. According to Happy, "John Wayne hates sham. This is his picture and he's determined to make it look right." He didn't want the set to appear artificial as it was to be filmed in Todd-AO, which showed every flaw, every nuance. But until those arrangements could be made, no definite agreement or schedules were to be finalized. "We scoured the border country for first-rate adobe-making practitioners," said Shahan. On the average, twenty-two makers were capable of mass-producing between three thousand five hundred and four thousand blocks daily. "We had to get Mexicans to make the adobe bricks," admitted Ybarra. "Adobe weighs forty pounds per brick, as against the eight pounds of our own bricks and is made by traditional methods strange to us. At one point we had fifty acres of bricks drying in the sun. You couldn't build a set like this out of plaster. Wind and rain would tear it apart. When we're finished with the movie, this set will stay here permanently. I'm told it will be a museum." Supposedly, laborers were brought across the border at Del Rio, taken to the ranch each morning and taken back at night.[43]

However, Brackettville resident Ralph Gonzales took exception to several of the aforementioned comments. "A local sixty-five-year-old gentleman was in charge of making the adobes. The adobe mixing was done with local people only, not with people from Mexico. When they had openings (for) labor, they made it a point to hire from Brackettville, to give the locals work. Myself and a lot of my friends, we made the adobe brick, but there was no one from Mexico." As for how many bricks were lying in the sun, well, that was another slight exaggeration. According to Ralph, "First of all, there were ten of us and we would nail two by fours and make all these squares on the ground. And we would pour the adobe mixture in each square. We had a total of six hundred squares, and we would cover all six hundred squares and then the next day we would (remove the squares and) do another six hundred. By the time they needed them, about four or five days later, they were dry enough to put them together and make walls out of them. That's what we had to look forward to every day. If I remember, they paid us $2.50 an hour." Utilizing a centuries-old traditional process, the bricks were manufactured with caliche (clay), manure, straw and water. Four giant plaster-mixing or cement-mixing machines were converted into adobe mixers. Straw was sprinkled in by hand. After being combined, the blend was dumped into wheelbarrows, transported to the work area, then pulled from the wheelbarrows and hand-packed into wooden forms. Once the thick oatmeal-type mixture set for awhile, the blocks were then removed from the forms and left to harden for five days in the Texas heat. Each adobe brick was seventeen inches by eleven inches by four and one half inches. After hardening, excess straw that stuck out all over the brick had to be shaved off with a small hatchet. To maintain an adobe block's integrity, it had to be used in construction within ten to fifteen days or the blocks would start to crumble. "If you use black dirt, you have to use a little manure in the recipe to make the adobe breathe," explained Happy. "Using the caliche, you can omit the manure. Horse manure is an important ingredient in making an adobe wall. If you can't get horse manure, then cow manure will have to do. It's pulverized and yet it makes the adobe wall 'breathe,' expand and contract with changing temperatures. If you don't put some kind of manure in there, the walls will sweat." So much caliche was quarried locally that, according to Wayne, a large pit "ten acres wide and fifteen feet deep" resulted from the digging in that area. Still visible today, the pit sits just across the road from the location of the faux Alamo church top about one-quarter mile due east of the Village. Physical inspection shows that at 120 x 240 x 140 x 350 feet, the pit is actually only three-quarters of an acre. A landing strip, no more than one thousand feet long, was located right across the road from both the caliche pit and faux top. Styrofoam blocks, identical in

"One of the forms used in making 1.25 million adobe bricks for the construction of the Alamo and old San Antonio..."

The "ten acres wide and fifteen feet deep" caliche pit is located next to the faux Alamo church top and directly across the road from the air strip.

size to the adobe blocks, were used in the re-construction of buildings and walls, which would be damaged by explosions. A wooden form used to pack the clay mixture and some of the Styrofoam blocks themselves can still be seen at John Wayne Museum in Alamo Village.[44]

During the course of the project, the weather became the enemy as bricks had to be re-made due to numerous storms. Torrential rains washed away thousands and thousands of blocks drying in the sun, literally dissolving them in the downpour. In one case, the rain was so severe that it washed a contractor's cement mixer several miles down East Pinto Creek. Furious thunderstorms caused a flash-flood on the West Nueces River, near Uvalde. Ranchers were advised to remove their livestock from bottom land, warned of low water crossings and notified that highways leading into the county would be closed. Las Moras Creek roared out of its banks on the morning of June 17, 1958, and sent almost five feet of muddy water racing through Brackettville. In addition to the Gateway Hotel, over sixty homes and twenty-five businesses were damaged by the flooding; Highway 90 east of town was closed down as well as Highways 674 and 344, north and northeast of Brackettville, and Highway 1572 at Spofford. A fifteen-foot wall of water rolled down the Nueces River. Just the day before, it was a dry river-bed. At least three deaths were blamed on the flooding in the Brackettville-Utopia-Sabinal area.[45]

"Ingredients are caliche (clay), straw, manure and water. When the mold is removed, the bricks bake in the sun for weeks."

As Al Ybarra recalled, "Four months after we started making bricks, Texas had a torrential rainstorm. (Six inches in twenty-four hours and over twenty inches during the month of June.) "The next morning the adobes were mush. Well, the day after the rain I went down and took a look at the telephone poles; the high water mark was six feet. If we'd built the set down here, it would've been…" One could only imagine. Belatedly, Shahan directed construction of a one-half-mile-long dike to reroute excess rainfall; a ridge of earth separating the creek from the village. Again, Ybarra commented on the damage: "Well, Happy had a bulldozer on the ranch, and he channeled the water away from where the set was gonna be. He worked for a couple of weeks, bulldozing dirt way, way away from it and building embankments to channel the water. And then, of course, we finally got started."

"The Alamo wasn't washed away. That was one consolation. Part of the walls of the quadrangle and part of the walls of the chapel were already up. Stone work on the front of the chapel was going to start the next week. The Alamo was set on higher ground and wasn't affected by the incredible downpour." Shahan continued almost philosophically, "1836 was a year of floods in Texas. So maybe nature is cooperating with us. I sure wish, though, that nature had spared me all those thousands

Over 1,600 adobe bricks drying alongside the Alamo chapel. At this stage of the set's construction, these bricks likely were used in the village of San Antonio. Once removed, the ground underneath the bricks was void of vegetation, which is evident in numerous scenes filmed in front of the Main Gate. Alamo Village Archives.

and thousands of adobes." The following week, much of the rain-damaged compound and chapel had been restored, but heavy rains left the area too wet to resume adobe-making activities. Concrete foundations had already been poured and adobe dwellings were being built when the rains came. Everything but the foundations was swept away by a creek that roared all but out of bounds during the hard storm. Rain damaged portions of the walls and about 60 percent of the chapel, as well as the face of the arch leading into the compound. "The arches in the chapel held, but the walls swelled and gave way, bringing everything down with them," Happy lamented.[46]

Once they started to make bricks again, another problem raised its smelly head. Believe it or not, they were running out of a key ingredient: manure! Too bad Dallas was so far away. During the Texas State Fair, it was estimated that over four million pounds of it would be removed from the fairgrounds. With forty men and four to six tractors pushing manure and loading it onto fifty dump trucks all day, well, that's a shitload of manure. During construction, delegates to a convention in Brackettville were taken to the set, where one woman asked Shahan how many adobe blocks had been made. "About seven hundred fifty thousand so far," replied Happy, "but there will be more than a million." When she asked what they were made of, he explained, "The first two hundred fifty thousand were made of hay, water, mud, manure and such." "What about the rest?" she asked. "Well," said Shahan, "we encountered certain shortages." Replied the woman, "You being a Texan, it must have been hay, water, or mud."[47]

This wasn't the first time Happy's property had been used for purposes other than ranching. In July 1943, the government had laid claim to eight thousand acres of his ranch, and ordered him to move his cattle out so the cavalry could use it for war maneuvers. As a good patriot, Shahan was glad to oblige. But when the soldier boys started using his water tower and windmill for target practice, it riled him a bit, and when they began cutting down his fences, well, it was more than he could take. Mounting his horse, he checked his .30-30 rifle and slowly rode to the gate that separated his pastureland from the army's reservation. A shaved-tail lieutenant galloped toward Happy and demanded entry.

"Don't open the gate," Happy advised.

"What's wrong with you?!" snapped the lieutenant.

"This is my land. There's no reason for you to cross it, so just turn around and head back."

"You can't stop the army," challenged the bold officer.

"Maybe not," replied Happy, leveling his rifle. "But I can stop you. Your men may mess up my pasture, but they're gonna have to ride over your body to get there."

Discretion being the better part of valor, the lieutenant tucked his tail between his legs and rode away. But this wasn't the end of it. Shahan later received a telephone call from an angry colonel:

"I can march my men anywhere I want, anytime I want!"

"If you march 'em on my land, bring a shovel and gravedigger."

That pretty much ended the discussion.[48]

With the cooperation of "Big" John Hamilton, Kinney County Judge Charles Veltmann, and the Commissioners Court, Happy and local businessmen A.H. Kreiger, C.C. Belcher, W.L. Moody IV, Tom Hurd and W.Z. Conoly formed a civic organization called Brackettville Enterprises (BE). As spokesman for the group, Happy had overall charge of the project. Shahan, Belcher, Moody, and Conoly were also members of the Rio Grande Co-op, which was charged with supplying power for construction and the movie location. Created as a focal point for all activities connected with construction of facilities for filming of the movie, BE would be involved in obtaining electrical power, inducting long-distance telephone arrangements, installing two-way radio communication and private telephone lines on location, planning for patrolling the area, and many, many other small but very important phases of production. Power lines and other discordant items had to be camouflaged and/or buried. Totally free from the markings of a jet-age civilization. "No fences, utility poles or paved roads (were apparent)," Ybarra noted happily. Once final arrangements were made, Batjac turned over plans to BE for construction but only after a guarantee that more than five hundred thousand homemade adobe blocks would be furnished for construction. Publicity at the time stated that approximately one mile of adobe walls of uniform shape, ten feet high and three feet thick, would be required.[49]

(According to Kreiger's son Alan, BE was just a sham organization. When Tom Hurd was questioned about it, he was said to reply, "Well, it doesn't matter if you stretch the facts a little." There may have been a consortium of local businessmen that coordinated activities, but Alan was sure that his father didn't have anything to do with it. A photograph was published in the June 1958 issue of *Texas CO-OP Power* that showed Moody, Conoly, Shahan, Hurd and Kreiger as they studied plans for the site. Alan alleged the photograph was false: "Tom Hurd, general manager of Rio Grande Electric, put it in there… (but) that's false. They didn't have a business that had anything to do with *The Alamo*. I think the whole thing was a complete fabrication." However, Kreiger did sell Batjac a workmen's compensation insurance policy for the construction of the set that his son thought was from the Commercial Union Insurance Company. This turned out to be a less than satisfactory experience because the company told Kreiger it would never again be involved in the film industry as "somebody was always fabricating a work comp claim everyday; falling down or something like that.")[50]

From October 1957 through the end of the year, BE obtained a water supply, finalized temporary living quarters for the workmen, began the manufacturing of adobe, and graded the location. The site selected for the Alamo set rested on top of a small rise, so the land had to be graded to maintain a gradual slope over one thousand feet to permit better filming of the various assaults on the Alamo. Giant dirt-moving machines sliced away from four to eight feet of soil in the process. Shahan seeded the newly level area with a number of grasses including buffel, blue panic, and bluestem to provide a natural look. Over four hundred acres of Happy's ranch would eventually be used to accommodate the movie set. Construction began with between three hundred and four hundred employees that Happy hired to augment his local crew. Wayne had already sent a core team of twenty individuals to supervise the materials and manpower for the construction program. Publicity exaggerated that set construction would cost between $1 million and $1.5 million and would eventually take almost two years before it was finished and filming began. However, in a March 22, 1960, Comparative Summary of Production Costs document, Batjac set construction costs were listed as only $184,678.89 and Shooting Operations Labor totaled $513,194.82.[51]

Because of the remote location, the construction site presented unique and expensive transportation problems. It was to cost almost $345,000 (not the $800,000 advertised) to transport cast, crew, and equipment to and from Brackettville. The permanent cast and crew of 342 individuals were housed at Fort Clark. There, bungalows had been refurbished before filming began. Each day, the company's sixty-four drivers, supervised by Transportation Director George Coleman, averaged more than fifteen hundred miles between the location and the company's headquarters at the Fort Clark Guest Ranch. Twenty cars and station wagons and thirty-four passenger buses were leased to accomplish this.[52]

Henry Fuentes, of Rio Grande Electric Co-op, explains how difficult it was to run power to the set. "I was with Rio Grande Electric," recalls Fuentes, "when Happy came by with Mr. Wayne. I was a part of the engineering department. So we were tickled to death to do whatever it was that was needed. Just, shortly after that, why, they both came in and Mr. Wayne had a couple of architects and some of his engineers there. They told us what they needed out there and we said, 'Well, let us study it a little bit.' So, based on the proposed load that they had quoted, we did a quick power requirements study. And, of course, we (already) had a line serving Happy's house. That line was a typical rural single-phase line. A single-phase line is a line that's got one hot wire and one neutral wire. The capacity of that line was at 7,200 volts. Well, based on what they told us, we concluded that that wouldn't do the job. So, we went in there and we rebuilt about fifty spans or fifty poles of line. We took that single-phase line and converted it from 7,200 volts; we added cross-arms to every pole; we added two additional conductors, and we converted that 7,200 to 12,500 volts, which gave the line the proper capacity. To serve the load in that immediate area, we talked to Mr. Wayne, and we said, 'Look, we don't guarantee anything unless we can build a small substation up there.' So we met up there with Happy and Mr. Wayne and they picked the site behind a small hill. We wanted the substation on the ground so it wouldn't be seen. But we built that substation behind a small hill and out of sight of the proposed Alamo structure. And got him what he needed up there in the way of capacity. As a matter of fact, I remember after we concluded our study, we started one weekend and we worked, just about overnight for a couple of days, but we got that line in there,

Electrical sub-station, c. 2014.

and we built the substation. The substation took a little while longer, but by now we had a line with capacity. And, of course, that tickled Mr. Wayne, and Happy was always warm to progress.

"Now, by the time that we built the small substation, there were crews out there doing all kinds of work. We had already done the line but we had to special-order the transformers that he needed. I used some of Wayne's crew to help pour a concrete slab to expedite things so we could put the transformers on it. It was seven of his crew that helped me. They worked, I mean they were good. Myself and another guy were putting the finish in the cement. And Happy came over there and he took these guys. And I thought, 'Well, I don't need them.' So, in a little while Wayne shows up. And he said, 'How's it going?' and I said, 'Fine. We'll be able to put this transformer on this slab in a couple of days.' He said, 'Where's the men that I sent you?' I said, 'Well, I don't know. Mr. Shahan come over here and got them.' Man, he took off. He was cussing when he left, he was cussing when he came back with Happy with the seven men. I said, 'Mr. Wayne. You know, we don't need them.' He said, 'I said they were going to be here. When you say they can go, then… Happy don't run this show. I do.' I said, 'Okay.' I'm in the middle of this thing. So, we just had those guys standing around until we got ready to leave."[53]

At that time an actual Mexican village would have consisted of numerous adobe buildings surrounding a central plaza. Ybarra's was more like a Western town, with the main structures facing a central dirt street including a hotel, cantina and church. Ybarra admitted years later that the appearance of the village was fictional: "I've seen enough of those old towns." In his words, they "represented a typical Mexican village of the 1830s." Just as Grant's script deviated from history when he changed the date of the death of Bowie's wife because "we decided to do this to improve Bowie's dramatic status," the authenticity of the (village's) layout was omitted purposely "(as)… most of the shooting will be close shots of building fronts, street scenes, entrances, and exits." If it was true that Ybarra researched the town and Alamo for over seven years before he started construction, one could assume that he had access to such research as the Sánchez-Navarro plan, the LaBastida map or the Greene B. Jameson plat, all of which would have clearly shown how the town and/or Alamo compound were laid out. (*Author's note*: Capt. José Juan Sánchez Navarro y Estrada was Adjutant Inspector of Nuevo Leon and Tamaulipas, and was present with Gen. Martin Perfecto de Cos in December 1835 when the Texian forces won the battle of Bexar. He was also there when Santa Anna's forces returned the following February. His plans encompassed the San Antonio River, the fortress as well as placement of Mexican batteries. Col. Ygnacio de LaBastida was commander of engineers of the Army of the North during the siege of the Alamo in March 1836,

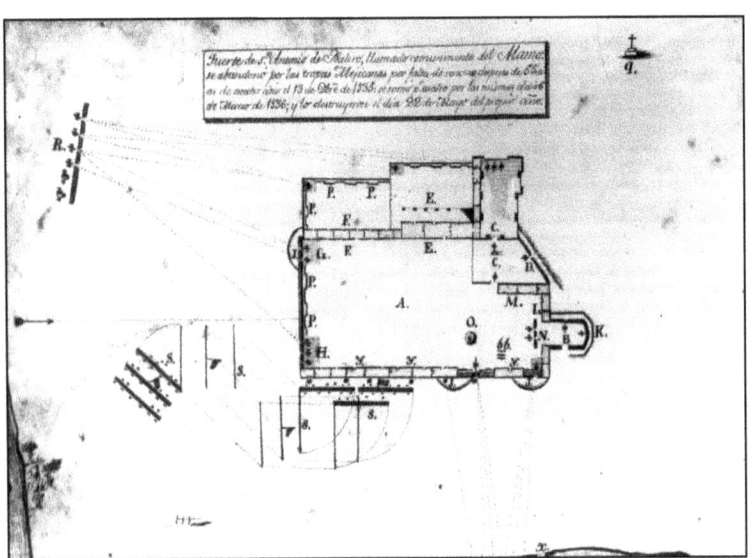

José Juan Sánchez Navarro y Estrada "Vista y plano del Fuerte del Alamo." Map of 1836 Alamo compound. Reprinted with the permission of the Daughters of the Republic of Texas Library.

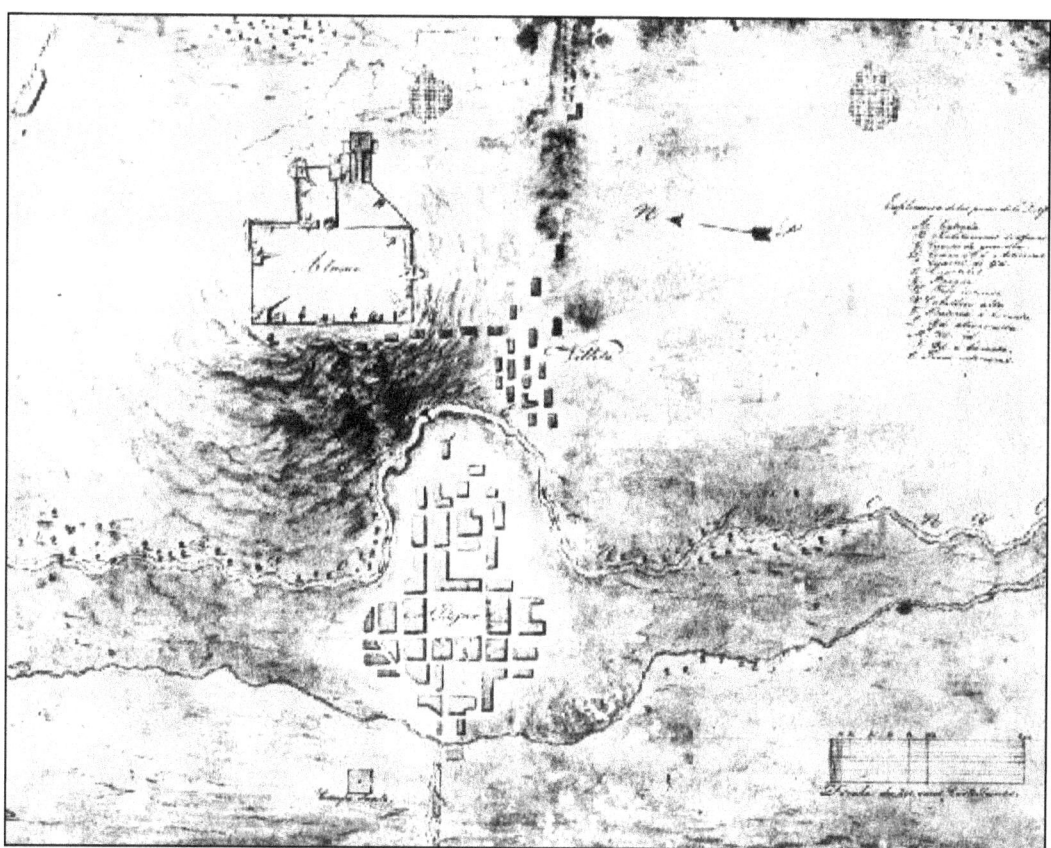

Ygnacio de LaBastida map of San Antonio de Bexar, 1836. Center of American History, University of Texas Austin collection. Reprinted with the permission of the Daughters of the Republic of Texas Library.

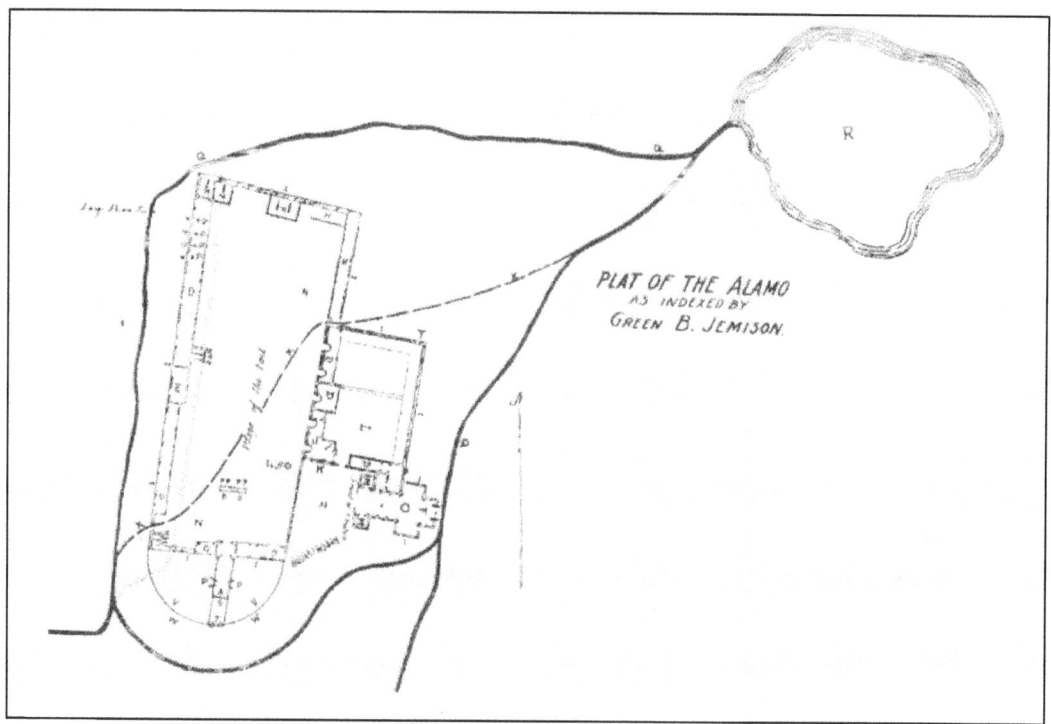

January 18, 1836, diagram of Alamo compound drawn by Green B. Jameson. San Antonio Light July 5, 1936. Reprinted with the permission of the Daughters of the Republic of Texas Library.

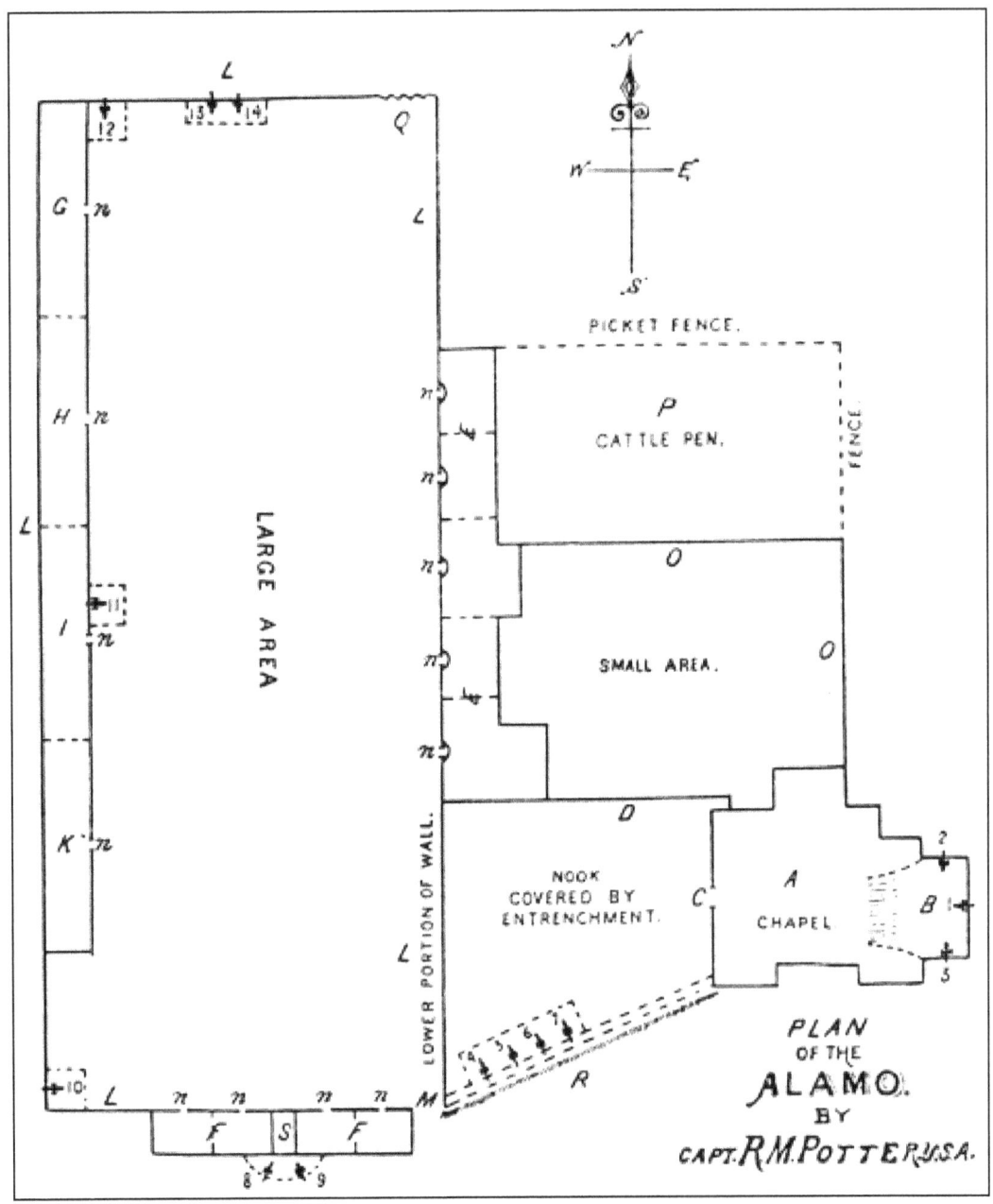

Reuben Marmaduke Potter's plat of Alamo compound, 1836.
Magazine of American History, January 1878, Vol. II, No. 1.

while Green B. Jameson was Chief Engineer of the Alamo garrison with the rank of major. Jameson's unmeasured diagram was limited to the Alamo compound itself; LaBastida's map, with graphic scale and compass, focused on the fortress and its environment. A topographical study of the immediate locale, it included the arrangement of streets and buildings in San Antonio proper as well as La Villita, with the identification of individual trees and cultivated fields.[54])

LaBastida's Bexar map shows both the Plaza de Isleta (Main Plaza) and the Plaza de Armas (Military Plaza), separated by the San Fernando Church. In fact, the town could be viewed as an inverted cross–quite different from the way that Ybarra laid it out. It's probable that Ybarra's choice of layout may have been deliberate as a very early draft of the script had a scene where the night before the final battle, Crockett and his love interest Chela (it was changed to Flaca in subsequent revisions) gaze at each other from afar, Crockett in the Alamo and Chela on the hotel porch. To have this unobstructed view, it would have been necessary to eliminate any structures in the way. The layout of a set is always designed as a direct response to the needs of specific scenes in a script. So, Ybarra deliberately planned it that way to have an open view between the hotel and the Alamo. He might have developed most of the layout for his Alamo compound from information derived from R.M. Potter's 1860 plat and perhaps Jameson's as well. (The latter plat was reproduced from a previous copy and was available in Amelia Williams' 1931 thesis as well as in a *San Antonio Light* article dated July 5, 1936. The original map was lost and has yet to be re-discovered.[55])

Potter's plat, though, did not locate Travis's headquarters on the west wall, which coincided with the construction of the movie set. Publicist Russell Birdwell touted in his massive news release that "sketches" by Jameson were located in Texan archives while an architectural plat made by an "un-named Mexican officer" were discovered in the Mexico City Museum. Everything mentioned by Birdwell needs to be accepted with caution as his press release also stated, "Every physical aspect of San Antonio de Bexar and the Alamo itself (were) established and faithfully recreated. The adobe buildings… are directly out of the context and fabric of actuality. The discovery of a location site exactly duplicate(d) the Alamo battlefield… Ybarra even made a quick trip to Spain to unearth the original plans of the Alamo… the plans (however) had been long lost or destroyed, though he was able to discover mission architectural designs in musty archives." Even Wayne wasn't averse to blatant publicity falsehoods; during the one-hour ABC Television special *Spirit of the Alamo*, broadcast on November 14, 1960, Duke stated, "That town down there; this wonderful old mission. We know we got them pretty close to right. We took the measurements from the old and original drawings and plans." None of this was factually correct though Ybarra did make several trips to San Antonio to physically measure the Alamo and, along with Nate Edwards and "Big" John Hamilton, took advantage of the research materials available in the Daughters of the Republic of Texas Library. The well-known but nevertheless untrue myth that Ybarra visited the archives in Madrid and uncovered the original construction drawings is also blatantly false. That claim was just publicity to hype the film's historical accuracy, which is woefully lacking. However Ybarra may

Frederic Ray 1955 aerial overview of the Alamo compound.

well have used Frederic E. Ray's aerial drawing–in the 1955 book *The Story of the Alamo*–because several details, including the three square buildings inside the south half of the west wall, appear nowhere else except in the Ray drawing.[56]

Nevertheless, Ybarra developed the basic Alamo ground plan used in construction. His original construction drawings, however, did not include any courtyard on the east side of the Long Barrack as evidenced in a photograph taken of the rear of the compound. There was just a short wall behind the arched entryway from the Campo Santo in front of the chapel so that the camera wouldn't see the open area in the background. The original set blueprints referred to this as a ten-foot by twenty-foot "wild wall" located about fifteen feet from the open archway. However, after production began and Wayne planned to film a scene in which the Tennesseans first view the Alamo, Ybarra created a back wall and a small Convent yard that changed the compound's original design, now setting it at an angle and eliminating the courtyard. There also were other structures built differently from what had initially been conceived in the blueprints: the chapel is smaller in the apse area and Travis's headquarters porch doesn't extend as far outward as originally intended.[57]

The reconstructed village of San Antonio de Bexar sat about three hundred yards north of the Alamo mission (opposite the latter's South Wall) instead of historically sitting about eight hundred yards due west of the mission (facing the West Wall). It should be noted that the movie version of the Alamo chapel faces in a different direction than does the actual Alamo in San Antonio. The real Alamo chapel faces due west, but the cinematic chapel faces east. As a result, dramatic dawn and dusk shots of the sun behind the Alamo were now possible. In essence, the entire movie set mission compound, including the chapel, was rotated 180 degrees from actual historical directions. (So as not to confuse the reader, all geographical descriptions of directions on the movie set are historical identifications.) According to Happy, there were two reasons why the Alamo movie set faced in the wrong direction. "One is we just shouldn't have faced it east," he said. "And the other… I just can't think of the other reason." Actually, one of the benefits of such a decision was to have a beautiful shot with Pinto Mountain in the background.[58]

Ybarra was trying to accommodate the landscape and natural lighting for the camera angles necessary to adequately film the various scenes. While the Alamo chapel was almost a full-size replica of the actual, the compound was deliberately constructed at 75 percent scale to accommodate the wide-angle dynamics of the Todd-AO camera. The lens would give proper depth perspective when viewed on film, so for that reason, all distances could be foreshortened, including the distance between the village and the Alamo. It enclosed a three-acre irregular trapezoid with the South Wall measuring *151 feet* wide and the North Wall *162 feet* wide while the north/south length of the compound along the West Wall was only *350 feet* long. (The actual movie set construction blueprints provided all these measurements and they are identified in *italics*, while all other comparative measurements are from primary historical sources.) Wide-angle dynamics dictated that the distances could be shortened so as to appear accurate. (The actual compound was 192 feet wide at the south end, 240 feet wide at the north end and almost 521 feet in length along the West Wall. Ybarra's Long Barrack also took advantage of this concept, measuring only *140 feet* long vs. the historical 192 feet, but his Low Barrack was actually fairly close to the original length: *131 feet* vs. *114 feet 7 inches*. Ybarra and his construction crew made detailed measurements of the Alamo chapel in San Antonio so as to recreate the structure inch-by-inch in Brackettville. The actual chapel is 62 feet 11⅜ inches across the front by 105 feet 8¼ inches outside length with an interior chancel width of 25 feet 2¾ inches, while the replica was *60 feet* by *84 feet 11 inches* with an interior width of *25 feet*.[59])

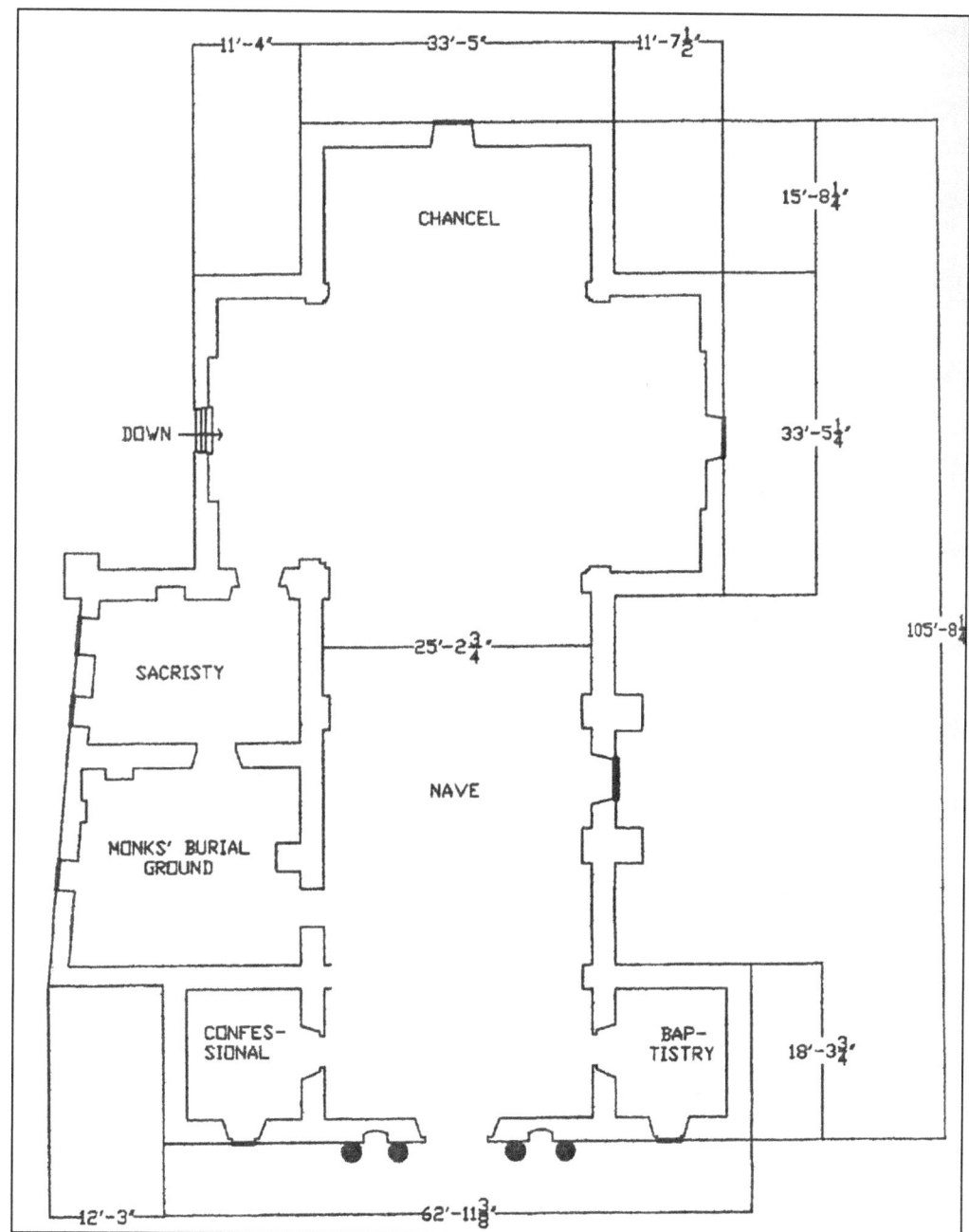

Mission San Antonio de Valero. Reprinted with the permission of John J. Farkis.

To better visualize the historical compound's layout, imagine a large rectangle standing vertically with the short sides of the rectangle on the top and bottom. The North Wall is at the top of the rectangle, the South Wall on the bottom, with the West and East sides of the compound on the left and right sides of the rectangle, respectively. In the rectangle's lower right corner is the Alamo chapel, sitting outside the southeast corner. It's connected to the lower right corner of the South Wall by a 110-foot-long wooden palisade at the southwest corner of the church and by an eighteen foot high adobe wall connecting to the Long Barrack at the church's northwest corner. This created an inner courtyard, which was the site of the old mission cemetery.

The South Wall was comprised mainly of a one-story structure known as the Low Barrack that was bisected by a two-leaved, wooden main gate. The gate's exterior was protected by a lunette (an exterior earthen fortification protruding from a wall) and an outer defensive ditch surrounding its parapet. Included in the barracks were a guardhouse to the west and two long rooms to the east, one of which may have been divided into two smaller rooms. James Bowie was said to have been killed in one of these rooms. An L-shaped portion of the barracks that included a kitchen and hospital extended to the north at the structure's eastern-most wing. Continuing in a northern direction is a low wall, separating the previously identified inner courtyard from the main plaza. This wall was unfinished in length and had a gap between it and the southern end of the Convento.

The two-story Convento, or Long Barrack, housed an armory on the first floor and hospital on the second. Just north of this was the one-story mission granary building, which was used as soldier's barracks. Completing the east side of the compound was a row of adobe and jacal houses also used as barracks for artillerymen. Just east of this (behind the Long Barrack) were the North Courtyard (or Cavalry Courtyard because it was part of a pen where horses and cattle were kept) and the Convento Courtyard (or Well Courtyard because it contained a well dug during the mission period to insure a water supply during sieges by hostile Indians). The northern courtyard also contained the mission's latrines. These eastern courtyards were formed by the ruins of what had originally been the outer walls of the convent cloister, as well as a northern courtyard adjacent to the cloister, which once housed a series of workshops of various types during the mission period including a weaving workshop, textile shops, pottery-making sheds, and an iron forge.

It has been suggested that the Alamo's North Wall, constructed primarily of adobe, stone and mud, was partially reinforced with a five-foot thick, eight- to nine-foot tall vertical timber-and-earth revetment or outer-work along its entire width that continued along the northeastern block of adobe structures. Others postulate horizontal cribbing braced at intervals by vertical posts. Regardless, the western 162 feet of the North Wall had no wooden revetment–horizontal, vertical or otherwise. In the eastern center of this wall was the *Fortin de Terán*, a twenty-four by fifty-four-foot, three-gun battery that featured two nine-pound cannons and one six-pounder and is the spot where tradition said Travis is believed to have died. Located at the northwest corner of the North Wall, a two-cannon, twenty-one by twenty-two-foot platform known as *Fortin de Condelle* was converted from the northern-most Castañeda building. To the east of the *Terán* battery were two Reyes buildings that joined the northeast corner of the plaza.

The West Wall consisted of a long series of stone rooms of varying conditions for its northern section and a single stone wall standing only about seven feet high for its southern section. The structures included a warehouse (alternately known as "hardware storage" or "artillery command") used to store material and tools to repair the garrison's artillery and gun carriages, the Trevino building (thought to be Travis' headquarters), two Castañeda buildings and two artillery embrasures. Connected by the ruined exterior walls of quarters previously used to house mission Indians, the buildings were used as officers' quarters during the Alamo siege. A twenty by twenty-four-foot earth and rubble elevated artillery platform, covered with wooden planking and revetted on the north and east side, was located at the southwest corner of the compound and built upon the remains of the Charli carpenter shop. Although only a little over four feet above ground, the platform held an eighteen-pound iron cannon, the largest of the Alamo's artillery contingent. *(For those interested in an extremely detailed analysis of the appearance of the Alamo at the time of the battle, Mark Lemon's "The Illustrated Alamo 1836–A Photographic Journey" is highly recommended.)*[60]

Ybarra went to some length to assure that the compound was historically correct, yet even the most cursory examination of the movie set would identify numerous significant inaccuracies. The following are some of the more obvious:

1. Travis's headquarters were located in the middle of the West Wall in the aforementioned Trevino building, identified as "Headquarters of the Alamo" on the Jameson map; the movie set placed his headquarters on the second floor of the Long Barrack so he'd literally be above the men he commanded. This is a continuing theme throughout the movie; the only time he addresses the men on an equal level throughout the entire movie is during the "Farewell address/faux Line in the Sand" scene.

2. There was neither a kitchen nor low wall constructed in front of the movie set's Alamo chapel. (The kitchen in the movie set was located on the first floor directly below Travis's headquarters in the Long Barrack.) There is some conjecture that the 1836 low wall actually represented the remains of the front of the mission's original chapel, the cornerstone of which was laid on May 8, 1744. Alas, the chapel, complete with tower and sacristy, was poorly constructed without structural stability, and eventually collapsed in 1749-50. By 1756, construction of the present Alamo stone chapel by master builder Hierónimo Ybarra and master sculptor Felipe Santiago began again. In 1758, the keystone was dated and set in place; however two planned bell towers were never constructed. Work ceased in 1772 at which time arches spanning the nave and the dome over the transepts had been completed. These arches were pulled down in 1835, the subsequent rubble then used to construct a long ramp and cannon platform at the eastern end of the chapel.

A headless statue, said to be that of San Antonio (St. Anthony), which may have stood in one of the Alamo niches. Reprinted with the permission of Ned Huthmacher.

A close-up photo of Wayne's Alamo statue niches. Note the shadow appearance of the statues in the niches.

3. None of the niches on the facing of the movie set's chapel held statues, which evidence indicates were there at the time of the actual battle. The niches in the lower level of the façade held the statues of San Francisco (St. Francis) and Santo Domingo. The statues of Santa Clara and Santa Margarita de Cortona that were to be located in the upper-level niches were unfinished. (A third-level niche was to contain a statue of Nuestra Señora de la Concepción.) Instead, sometime after 1793, someone purchased or paid for the carving of San Fernando and San Antonio (St. Anthony) and placed them in the upper niches of the chapel façade. Ybarra solved this problem by painting silhouettes of the statues in his niches. The profile of Wayne's chapel has the slight appearance of the long-distinctive "humped" gable, or bell-shaped parapet, which was designed by architect John Fries and added to the Alamo by the U.S. Army in 1850. Ybarra initially designed the ridgeline of the chapel to be relatively flat but Wayne protested. Rather, he indicated he wanted the unique look so viewers would have a connection between the historical Alamo and movie set. In addition to the second-story windows shown on the movie Alamo structure, which were not present in 1836, Ybarra had also placed a small white cross on top of the chapel.[61]

4. The scrollwork around the mission door and niches, as well as the four columns that adorn the face of the building, was molded by Redondo Manufacturing, a San Antonio firm. The company had been allowed to make plaster castings of the Alamo's actual "Tuscan" style columns in 1936, and the molds were still available. The columns were made of concrete, but when set in place, inadvertently were reversed; the spirals in the columns rotated in the opposite direction from the original chapel. By the time it was noticed, filming was already under way. According to Ybarra, he didn't think anyone would catch it. Interestingly, Ybarra's original 1951 blueprint also showed reversed spirals on the columns.[62]

A close-up of Wayne's Alamo façade. Note the reversed spirals on the columns on either side of the lower statue niches. The direction on each and every column should be reversed.

5. Ybarra constructed the fortification of the main gate of the movie set without the lunette. A U-shaped structure typically built on the outside of a military compound, it consisted of two rows of upright cedar logs with packed dirt between them and featured an earthen berm or parapet between the logs and surrounding ditch. It also contained a sally port–or narrow gap–between the logs, which allowed access to the main gate. This gap was on the western face of the lunette, restricting direct access into the compound through the main gate. Since archaeological digs in San Antonio have proved that the 1836 military plats accurately represented the original lunette, it has subsequently grown in size in our creative awareness into a formidable fortification extending over sixty feet out from the gate–far bigger than imagined in the 1950s. So Wayne and Ybarra can be excused for not including it at all.[63]

6. The movie did not show evidence of a cannon ramp inside the mission church. General Martin Perfecto de Cos had arrived in San Antonio on October 9, 1835, and taken command of the Mexican garrison at the Alamo. Aided by Colonel Ugartechea, Cos immediately began fortifying the mission by strengthening the outer walls and adding fifteen cannons to its arsenal. Inside the chapel, engineers used material from six collapsed roof arches, a large section of the East Wall, and stone and rubble from the Convento courtyard, to

John Wayne directs Laurence Harvey in a scene from the film as Richard Widmark looks on. Note the absence of a cannon ramp or platform in the rear of the chapel. Rather than show rubble from the collapsed roof arches, Wayne used fallen timber. The two large telephone poles are support for and ladders to the forward cannon platform.

construct a seventy-four-foot ramp leading from the entrance of the chapel to its rear wall as well as for the base of a twenty-five by twenty-four-foot cannon platform. Earth from nearby entrenchments and the nearly six hundred-foot-long section of acequia that Cos had re-routed west of the West Wall, was used to fill in between the rubble and as a top-coat upon which a wooden ramp was laid. Vertical timbers were used for scaffolding, revetted on each side, to further brace and support the ramp. Referred to as *Fortin de Cos*, a three twelve-pound cannon battery was placed on the platform, facing east. It is believed that during the siege, Almeron Dickinson, James Bonham, Gregorio Esparza and others manned this position.[64]

7. The set's outer adobe walls varied in height from nine to twelve feet and were a minimum of thirteen inches thick, while the original Alamo compound walls varied from seven to twelve feet high and were two-and-a-half to three feet thick. An assistant saw the walls and suggested to Ybarra they be built slightly higher. Wayne said no, "I want to see thousands behind every wall." As the walls required a certain amount of stability, they were strengthened with buttresses. Most of the Ybarra/Hernandez adobe bricks measure seventeen by eleven by four and one half inches. Sometimes Ybarra had Chato lay them lengthwise, giving a wall with a thickness of thirteen or fourteen inches. But the Alamo "South" and "West" walls were laid perpendicular to the length of the wall, rendering a wall eighteen or nineteen inches

thick. Long Barrack walls were laid lengthwise, making the walls thirteen to fourteen inches thick as are the back walls of the rear courtyard.[65]

8. The South Wall palisade was constructed too low in height compared to its actual dimensions. Historically, it was believed that the palisade was a 110-foot-long stockade wall, about seven to eight feet in height, built of two rows of cedar logs, placed six-feet apart, packed with fill, with a berm and ditch on the outside, similar to the lunette. The Sanchez-Navarro plat suggests that it was protected on the outside by an abatis, a wall made of trees, cut down and placed side by side with the entangled, sharpened branches pointed toward the attackers, in addition to a trench. Recent archeological excavations now suggest a single row of vertical posts with an interior earthen firing step or banquette almost two feet high with loopholes cut about four and one-half feet from the step. Positioned about halfway along this palisade was a two-foot high, fifteen by twenty-four foot earthen platform upon which a four-pound cannon fired through an embrasure in the logs. The movie set palisade was only about sixty-five feet long and three- to four-feet high. It consisted of a single row of posts, without a trench or outer works. The right center of the palisade consisted of gabions, which were large baskets made of woven sticks and filled with rocks and earth. An actual 18th Century fortification technique, Batjac used them to fill the gaps in the palisade while allowing heavy equipment to be brought onto the film set. When necessary, the gabions were moved by forklifts. Ybarra's original blueprints showed two rows of cedar

Removable rock- and dirt-filled gabions (baskets). A timber post palisade can be seen on either side of the gabions. Due to its irregular height, a flat board was placed on top of the timbers to protect horses as they jumped over the palisade during the battle scenes.

posts, eight to ten inches in diameter, separated by five feet of fill dirt, but by the time the set was constructed that concept proved ill-conceived. During one of Wayne's frequent inspections, he noticed Ybarra had already built the palisade and yelled, "What the hell were you thinking of? You know we can't have that wall up yet—the first scene doesn't call for it. Take the damn thing down." Ybarra patiently explained that, rather than having a stationary structure, it was designed so it could be moved when necessary to allow large movie equipment trucks to enter and exit the compound during shooting. A shallow trench was excavated, and palisade stakes were set in place; if the palisade wasn't needed, the stakes were pulled, the ditch covered with boards, and the boards with dirt. Quick, convenient, and efficient. Wayne just smiled.[66]

Ybarra's workers built the outer perimeter of the compound first, followed by the chapel. Concrete footings, twenty-four inches wide and four inches deep, laid out the rough dimensions of the rectangle. The construction crew started with the Low Barrack, which included the round arched main entrance, then worked their way counter-clockwise up the Long Barrack East Wall, across the North Wall, down the West Wall and finally connecting once again with the Low Barrack in the southwest corner. As previously mentioned, the low wall enclosing the Campo Santo in the front of the chapel was omitted.

The following series of photographs document the construction process of the Alamo compound and its buildings. Once the ground was leveled, wooden two-by-fours were used to construct the forms for concrete footings of the northwest corner of the compound. In the background staging area are row after row of adobe bricks to be used once the footings are ready. Alamo Village Archives.

Wheelbarrows poured a mixture of cement and stones into West Wall forms that were then leveled and smoothed. Alamo Village Archives.

Workers inspect the West Wall footings. The village of San Antonio will be constructed along the line of trees at the far left. Alamo Village Archives.

Sand, cement, stone and mud are used in the construction process. Alamo Village Archives.

Two workers set the next course of adobe blocks on the wall of an interior room. Alamo Village Archives 2300-03.

Abode craftsmen position bricks into place along the West Wall while additional bricks are unloaded from a truck. Rows of bricks drying in the sun can be seen in the background. Alamo Village Archives 2300-01.

The rubble-filled East Wall/northeast corner of the Alamo compound. Alamo Village Archives.

Construction of the West Wall. The North Wall is almost complete absent the northwest cannon ramp. Alamo Village Archives.

The construction process appeared to be identical throughout the project: after the footings were laid, large telephone poles towering over thirty feet high were set into the ground, providing a crosscheck to which the adobe bricks would be laid. The posts served a multi-purpose: not only were they a visual part of the structure, but they also guaranteed a straight line, assuring both the perpendicularity and structural integrity of the façade. You can see evidence of one of the posts in the scene when Bowie meets Travis climbing down the ladder pole in the chapel from the cannon platform. The ladder appears to have the rungs attached by rope and/or rawhide. (Both the platform and ladder were eventually removed in the late 1970s due to safety precautions. Prior to that, Happy had removed the lower eight feet of rungs and encircled the pole with barbed wire to discourage visitors from climbing to the platform.) Since most of the major structures had large poles in each of the four corners, they had to be hidden by artificial buttresses. The buttresses also helped support the relatively thin wall structure although not present in the original structure. In the same aforementioned scene, you can also see the back wall of the chapel. Historically, there should have been a cannon ramp leading from inside the open doorway to the back wall. This feature would not be added to the movie set until the filming of *Alamo–The Price of Freedom* in 1987. At that time a new apse was also created. For Wayne's film, all that's present inside the mission chapel is timber, rubble and a collapsed roof structure. Ybarra personally painted the interior walls, adding what he believed to be typical religious symbols.[67]

Construction on the South Wall Main Gate.

Exterior view of the South Wall. The buttresses supported the walls and also added an aesthetic touch. Alamo Village Archives.

Interior of the South Wall. The wooden stairway to the roof has not yet been added nor has the southwest cannon ramp.

Photograph of the Alamo compound taken from the North Wall. Two wooden Long Barrack staircases have been completed in addition to the one near the Main Gate. Note that the squared-off top of the South Wall has been changed to a more angular appearance. Alamo Village Archives.

Construction of numerous rooms along the West Wall.

The West Wall has now been plastered and whitewashed. A cedar post ramada has also been erected. Jornos will eventually be placed under its roof. Alamo Village Archives.

The facings of the buildings were covered with plaster, textured and painted as required. Later, the plaster was artistically chipped off here and there to reveal the adobe brick, making the buildings appear old. Dirt piled on top of adobe walls streaked the sides whenever it rained, which gave it an authentic appearance. "Adobe is actually fine construction," Ybarra pointed out. "It is naturally insulated and when kept properly, will last forever." He noted there was a tremendous amount of painting that needed to be done. "What the hell. If I paint this whole set, I'll need $5,000 worth of paint. So I talked with my Mexican foreman about whitewashing the whole thing. In other words, we put pigment in the washtub. I had fifty gallon sacks of it, mixed in with water, and I get the colors I want. I don't think I spent $150 on pigments. The buildings were finished so close to the start of shooting that we didn't have time to go around and spray them for antiquity. And I put dirt on the top of all the buildings, washed it down, and it looked natural." In addition, chemicals from a hose were sprayed on various structures to give them a streaked appearance. Local resident and extra Tim Cumiskey recalls, "When they first built the structures out there, they were so white you couldn't even look at them; the sun was so bright that you couldn't even see. When the special effects guys came in, they all had a sledge hammer in one hand and a spray, backpack-type, water canister-type thing, like a bug sprayer-type thing, and they would come along, and they would put an adobe brick on top of the wall, and then they'd go around and slam that hammer into the wall and then make the adobe run down the side there to make it look old. By the time they got done, it looked like it had been sitting there for two hundred years."

The Long Barrack has now been plastered, streaked and chipped to give it an aged appearance.

Nails used in construction were artificially rusted so that the heads would not shine and show up in the movie. Here and there, cactus grew out of the walls, corn-cribs were placed strategically around the compound to give it a sense of authenticity, and tree trunks were hollowed out to serve as water troughs. Ybarra also dug an acequia or aqueduct that wound its way from the base of the hill facing the "North Wall," under the parapet where the breach was made, down two-thirds the length of the plaza and then out a port in the "West Wall" next to Bowie's room. Much of the wood used was said to come from native timber found on the Shahan ranch with many of the doors and windows salvaged from buildings at Fort Clark. As many of these doors were not of standard size, doorways had to be custom-made to accommodate them. To obtain age-appropriate fixtures, Ybarra traveled to Mexico and brought back old handmade iron hardware. On one of Duke's frequent visits, he noticed the walls were bare and white, so he instructed Ybarra to "Put something in the walls." Designs were added "to give it character, for the sake of the camera."[68]

The next series of photographs detail construction of the Alamo chapel. Once concrete footings have been formed, telephone poles were set in place to assure structural integrity and perpendicularity. Note that in this photo poles have been set for both the church and Travis's headquarters. The first eight courses of adobe bricks have been laid around the perimeter of the chapel. The arch enclosing the front entrance has also been erected as has the wall connecting the church to Travis's headquarters. Alamo Village Archives.

The Alamo chapel façade was one of the last edifices built on the set. Working from measurements, photographs, and molds, Ybarra tried to make the chapel as accurate as possible. "We have to know where and how the action took place before we can make the place for it to happen in the film," Ybarra explained. "We have built them (the Alamo buildings) from measured drawings of the original Alamo. They are as faithfully and accurately reproduced, inch by inch, as any replica could be." In fact, the church was the only building that wasn't entirely made of adobe. Although the stories vary, depending upon the recollections of those telling them, everyone agrees that the front of the church was a three- or four-foot-thick wall, built of quarried limestone from Brackettville. Ybarra indicated that one day while driving to town, he noticed a road construction crew with several dump trucks loaded with rock that had been blasted out of a nearby hill where a new road was being constructed. Although not perfect, the limestone was a close enough match to the original façade and Ybarra negotiated with the road crew to use it. He then sent his own crew over to haul the stone away for free. Ybarra added, "I sat in front of the chapel and supervised the placing of each stone. It was the most important building on the set, and I wanted to make sure it was perfect." Happy, though, said he thought this limestone came from a razed building at Fort Clark. Others believe it came from a demolished building in downtown Brackettville. That building's foundation is still visible, located to the right of FM 674 as you drive out of town toward Alamo Village. The building faces the street and sits one block past the main stoplight. A close-up viewing of construction photos, however, appears to validate Ybarra's account: all blocks are irregular in form and massive in size.[69]

The wall from the church to Travis's headquarters is now almost complete. Alamo Village Archives.

Further along in set construction. The South Wall/Main Gate is finished, walls start to enclose the chapel and Long Barrack. Alamo Village Archives 2300-04.

A workman searches for just the right stone for the four-foot thick façade. Three interior arches have now been erected, while two rooms on either side of the doorway are being built. Alamo Village Archives.

Limestone blocks for the façade are placed in position. The interior of the chapel and adjoining walls are plastered and whitewashed. Alamo Village Archives.

The remains of an adobe building on Ann Street from which, it is said, limestone was used for the façade, 2008.

The Alamo façade nears completion. Lower-level windows have been completed, columns on either side of the doorway are in place, albeit with spirals rotated in the wrong direction.

Alfred Ybarra inspects blueprints in front of the Alamo chapel. Alamo Village Archives.

The Alamo chapel façade is almost complete. Recessed arches have been installed in the upper statue niches. Cedar posts and a roof over the kitchen of the Long Barrack can be seen at the far left. At this point of the process, the wooden palisade is still missing.

Initial construction on the wall between the chapel and Long Barrack. The church footer trenches are being excavated; telephone poles are absent as the walls are not yet complete. The inside of the North Wall, complete with buttresses can be seen at the far right. Alamo Village Archives.

The next series of photographs details the construction process of the Long Barrack/Travis's headquarters. Construction of the first level of the Long Barrack. Again, telephone poles were used to assure structural integrity. Alamo Village Archives.

Construction of the upper level of the structure. The building is now plastered and whitewashed but still needs to be textured and chipped. Alamo Village Archives.

A view of the side and rear of Travis's headquarters; although the stairs leading to the second floor have been completed, the roof remains uncovered. The finished West Wall can be seen on the far left. Alamo Village Archives.

The almost-finished, whitewashed headquarters building. Window frames and louvered doors have yet to be added. Alamo Village Archives.

One section of the two-story Convento was initially intended to be finished in appearance as close to historically accurate as possible. However, in fact, nothing of this structure resembles the original. All rooms in this building other than Travis's upstairs headquarters, Mrs. Dickenson's downstairs kitchen and Smitty's sick room were used as actors' dressing rooms. Other than the interior sets and Wayne's office building, this was the only building that had air-conditioning. All adobe buildings were covered with whitewashed plaster, with light blue trim painted around bottoms, doors and windows.[70]

Happy wasn't the only Shahan involved in the construction process; since his wife, Virginia, had horticultural aspirations, Wayne enlisted her help landscaping the set. "In the yards and houses in the village supplementing the main set of the Alamo," she explained, "we want to have colorful blooming plants—bright yellows and reds and blues. This during September, October and November, when the camera crews will be shooting." She requested that the community pitch in to help landscape Old San Antone. "We also wish to have some kind of vine growing on the walls of the Alamo compound. If people want to send seeds, I shall be very grateful. But their advice on what to plant and when, will be welcome too." All submissions were to be sent to Mrs. J.T. "Happy" Shahan at Brackettville. No other address was necessary. Usually, a member of the set decoration department called a "greensman" was responsible for selecting, purchasing, and placing all appropriate greenery. Obviously, the land was stripped naked in order to build the various sets, but vegetation would have grown back by the start of production. Virginia's efforts and those of the local community helped augment nature.[71]

A view of the Alamo chapel and Long Barrack from the roof of the South Wall. Note the small white cross over the chapel's parapet. This would later be replaced by the iconic "fallen" cross. Alamo Village Archives 2462-14.

Aerial view of the Long Barrack and Alamo chapel. You can clearly see the roof over the rear porch of the headquarters, the covered Convento courtyard and the fallen wooden roof of the chapel. A flagpole mound has been constructed and the wooden palisade, complete with gabions, is now in place.

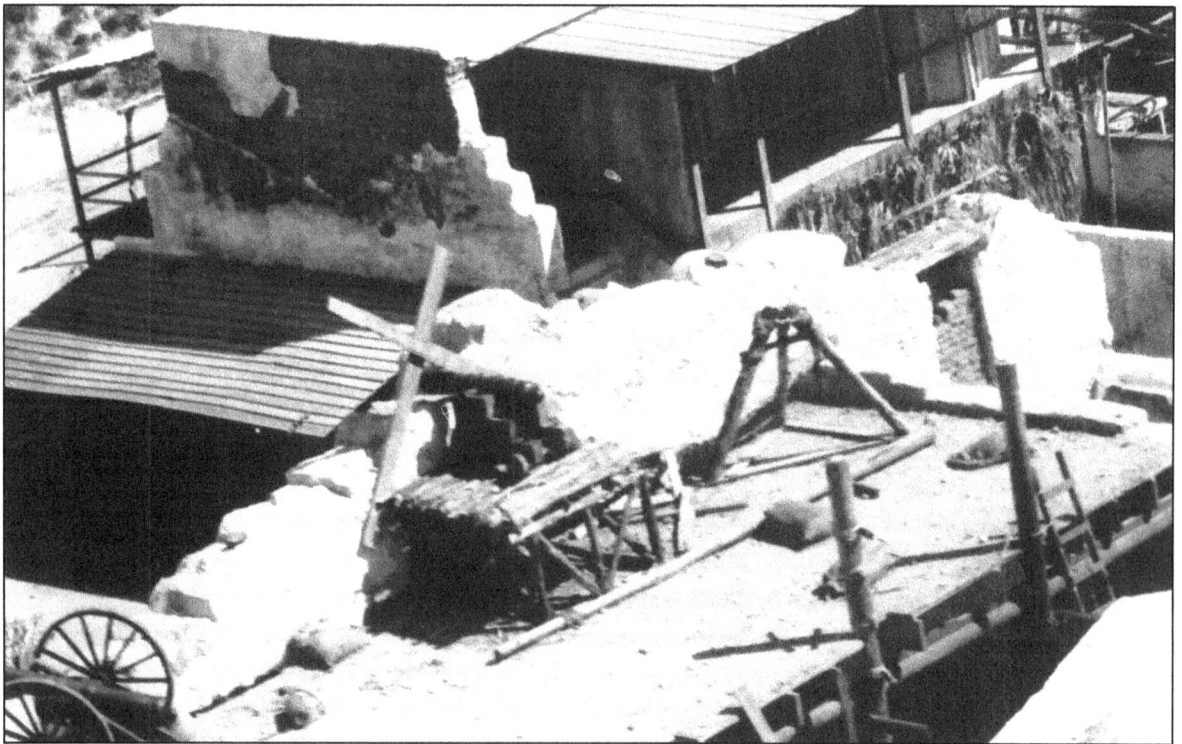

An aerial close-up of the rear of Travis's headquarters and the back of the Alamo chapel parapet. A cannon, sitting on two wooden blocks, can be seen at the far left, while the "fallen" cross is wedged between a wooden platform and the back of the parapet.

An aerial close-up of the rear of the Long Barrack. Numerous scaling ladders lean against the West Wall; ramadas were built behind the Long Barrack and along the West Wall. Bowie's "death scene" room in the chapel is visible in the lower left portion of the photograph.

An interior view of the Alamo compound. The cattle corral is visible on the right; a white jorno can be seen through the corral rails. Alamo Village Archives 2462-11.

A view of the cattle corral and West Wall taken from the northeast corner of the compound. The burning tree visible in the scene where dragoons enter the compound during the final battle action is on the far left. Alamo Village Archives 2462-15.

A view of the Long Barrack, corral, and South Wall taken from the cannon platform on the North Wall.

An interior view of the compound taken from the northwest cannon emplacement. The small white cross can be barely seen on the Alamo chapel. The buildings have been plastered but not yet aged or chipped. Alamo Village Archives 2462-13.

A reflective Alfred Ybarra gazes out on his finished set. White jornos were constructed under the ramada along the West Wall.

A view of the Alamo compound taken from the southwest cannon ramp. The ramada in the previous photograph can now be seen in its entirety. Alamo Village Archives 2300-06.

Soon it became apparent Wayne was suffering from serious financial woes as he was dangerously close to shutting down construction of the movie set. He was forced to buy out Robert Fellows–the result of a separation of the Wayne-Fellows partnership several years earlier–and thus didn't have enough money to pay his workers. Recalled Happy Shahan, "I remember one time in 1958 that Wayne called me and said, 'Stop building.' I said, 'Why?' 'Because I don't have any money.' I said, 'Are you going to shoot this picture?' He used a few choice words saying, 'You know we're going to shoot this picture!' I said, 'Well, if you're going to shoot the picture, we better not stop building.' He said, 'I told you; I don't have any money!' 'Hey,' I said, 'we got to keep building. I'm coming to Hollywood.' 'Well, it won't make any difference,' he said. 'I don't have any money to continue.' I told him I would be out there the next day which I was. Before I left, I went to the bank and got me a ($100,000) note. I told them at the bank to make it out to John Wayne and Happy Shahan, John Wayne's name first, and I'd sign it at the bottom. Then I went out to Hollywood and told Wayne, 'Hey, we're going to keep building, you sign this note. When we get the money, we'll pay them. You'll be better off and I'll be better off, and you won't have to worry about anything.'" Happy reminded Duke that if he lay off three hundred to four hundred workers then, it would result in a major problem in the future because "you can't just re-hire them at the drop of a hat." They had to find other employment somewhere, and chances are they wouldn't be available when "you" needed them again. "I went out and ate with him that night," continued Shahan, "and, in fact, he took me to his home. We argued a good part of the evening, which was not unusual for us. But, you know, after he got to thinking about it, he realized it wasn't a bad deal. We just kept building the sets. And it wasn't a bad deal for me. I said, 'Here's what we'll do. I'm going to complete this town set for *The Alamo* and that will be my money. You have to agree not to destroy the town. *The Alamo* set is your money; you can destroy anything you want there.' So everything worked out. I got a town, and he got his picture. *The Alamo* sets weren't intact, of course. He blew the hell out of them at the end of the picture. It cost me a million dollars to put the *Alamo* set back together again." Wayne accepted the proposal and work never halted. Happy later said that when Wayne filmed the explosion of the powder magazine in the Alamo chapel, Michael Wayne turned to him and said, "Well, Shahan, there goes your Alamo." Happy smiled and replied, "No sir. That was *your* Alamo. The town's mine."

"Whenever Wayne ran out of money, Happy would take care of it," said Virginia Shahan. "He would go down to the bank and get a loan. He would cover the payroll, bills, etc. Whatever was needed. He was good for it and Wayne would repay it." Wayne had a slightly different memory of all this. "The production manager made a bad mistake," Duke said. "When we first went down, we planned to use ordinary false-front sets for the town and the shell of the Alamo. Then we figured the cost of the trailers to house actors and crew and got around to the idea of putting up buildings instead. We put dressing rooms in some buildings, used others for warehouses. So we came up with something we hadn't intended, and before we got through we'd built a town. We built magnificent corrals for the horses and drilled two wells." Wayne had initially intended to have just three complete structures in the town set: the church, cantina and hotel. All remaining structures were to be two-walled sets. "Wild walls" were placed in several structures as well: the back of Mrs. Dickenson's kitchen in the Alamo compound, Flaca's hotel room window, and the back of Travis's headquarters. In the latter, the camera was located on a back extension of the floor, looking into the room. "Wild walls" are movable partitions that can be positioned wherever necessary to simulate space, rooms and hallways, yet allow camera and lighting set-ups to be made that otherwise wouldn't be possible. They can be used in scenes where room dimensions and/or ceiling height limitations make filming impractical. In essence, they provide more space for filming. According to Michael Wayne, "There were no studio sets. The Alamo was constructed in its entirely so that we could film anywhere in it. All the rooms were designed so that you could be outside, go through the door, and you were in a room designed so filming could take place. It was actually cheaper than renting space at a studio."[72]

All of the following information comes from Russell Birdwell's press releases and newspaper articles written at the time. In addition to the building of the two principal sets, the construction crews installed more than ten miles of underground wiring, both electrical and telephonic. Road crews built a total of fourteen miles of heavy-duty gravel (450 truckloads) and tar roads. To supply the cast and crew with water, and to create a flowing river where none had ever existed, a special well-digging crew brought in six deep wells, capable of producing more than 25,000 gallons of pure artesian water each day. This included a 135-foot deep well with a 25,200-gallon reservoir. Built at a cost of $5,000, it was estimated that over one million gallons of water would be used during the filming. Modern toilet facilities, with more than five miles of sewage lines, were installed as a permanent part of the location buildings. Five thousand trees and shrubs were planted to replicate the appearance of the terrain at the original site. Knowing that the small town of Brackettville couldn't possibly accommodate the large cast and crew that were to accompany the project, Wayne leased property at Fort Clark and workers were hired to refurbish the officer's barracks as well as the mess hall, so that everyone could be housed and fed.[73]

More than one million square feet of lumber, forty miles of reinforced construction steel, one hundred twenty-five thousand square feet of concrete flooring (six carloads of cement), twelve miles of water pipe and more than thirty thousand square feet of imported Spanish tile roofing went into the Alamo project, as well as thousands of dollars worth of miscellaneous building materials such as forty kegs of nails, wiring, lathe, three thousand sacks of plaster, two hundred gallons of paint, fifteen thousand square feet of corrugated iron roofing, and twelve hundred railroad ties used for beams. Workmen installed more than $75,000 worth of portable air-conditioning equipment both on the set and in the living quarters of the cast and crew. A four thousand-foot landing strip was constructed to rush the film dailies back and forth to Hollywood–it's located right across the road from the faux Alamo top and caliche pit. More than five thousand cedar posts were brought in to create the seventeen hundred acres of stock corrals necessary to quarter the saddle horses, work horses and mules used in the production of the movie.[74]

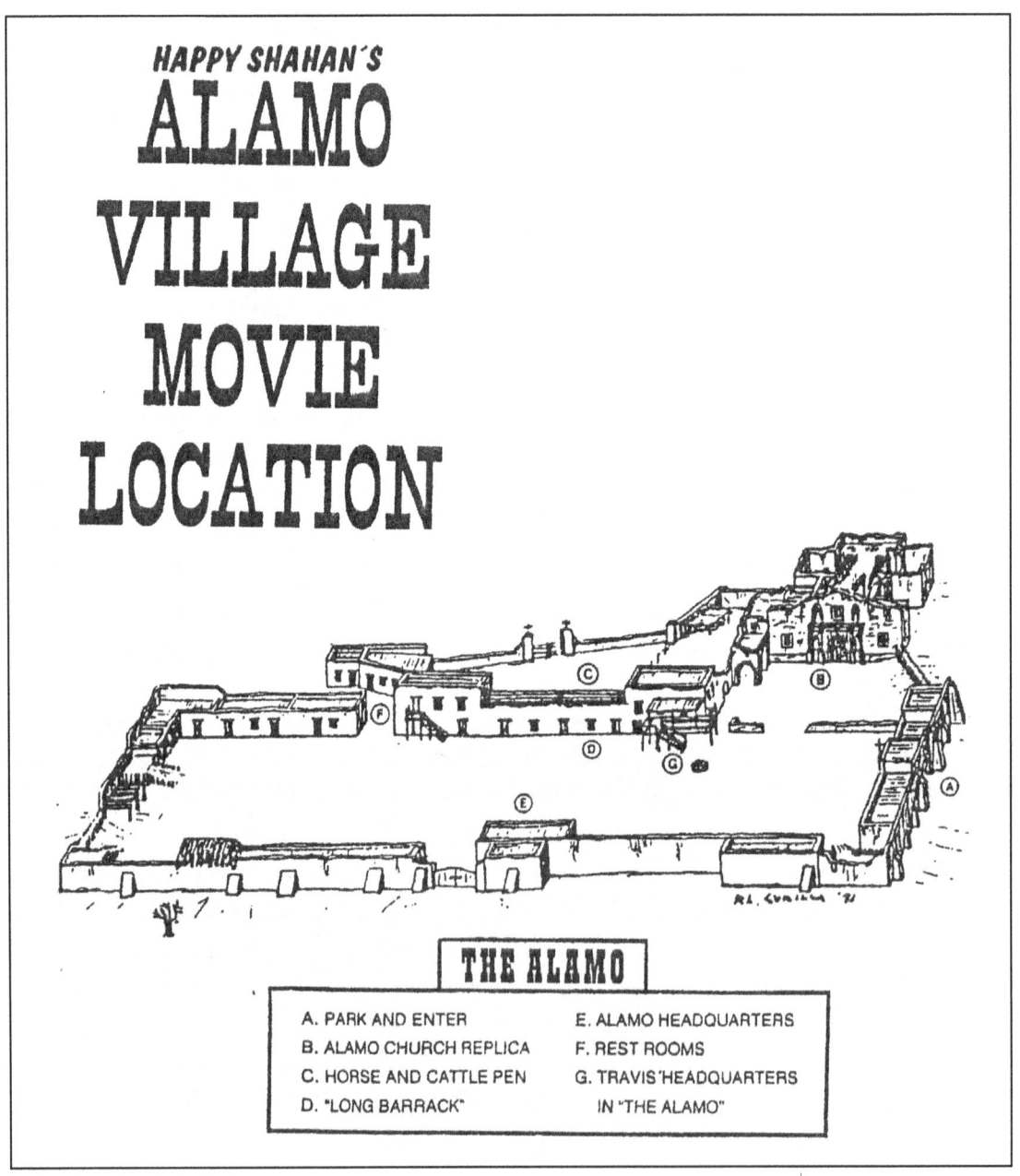

Alamo Village brochure, Alamo Compound, c. 2001.

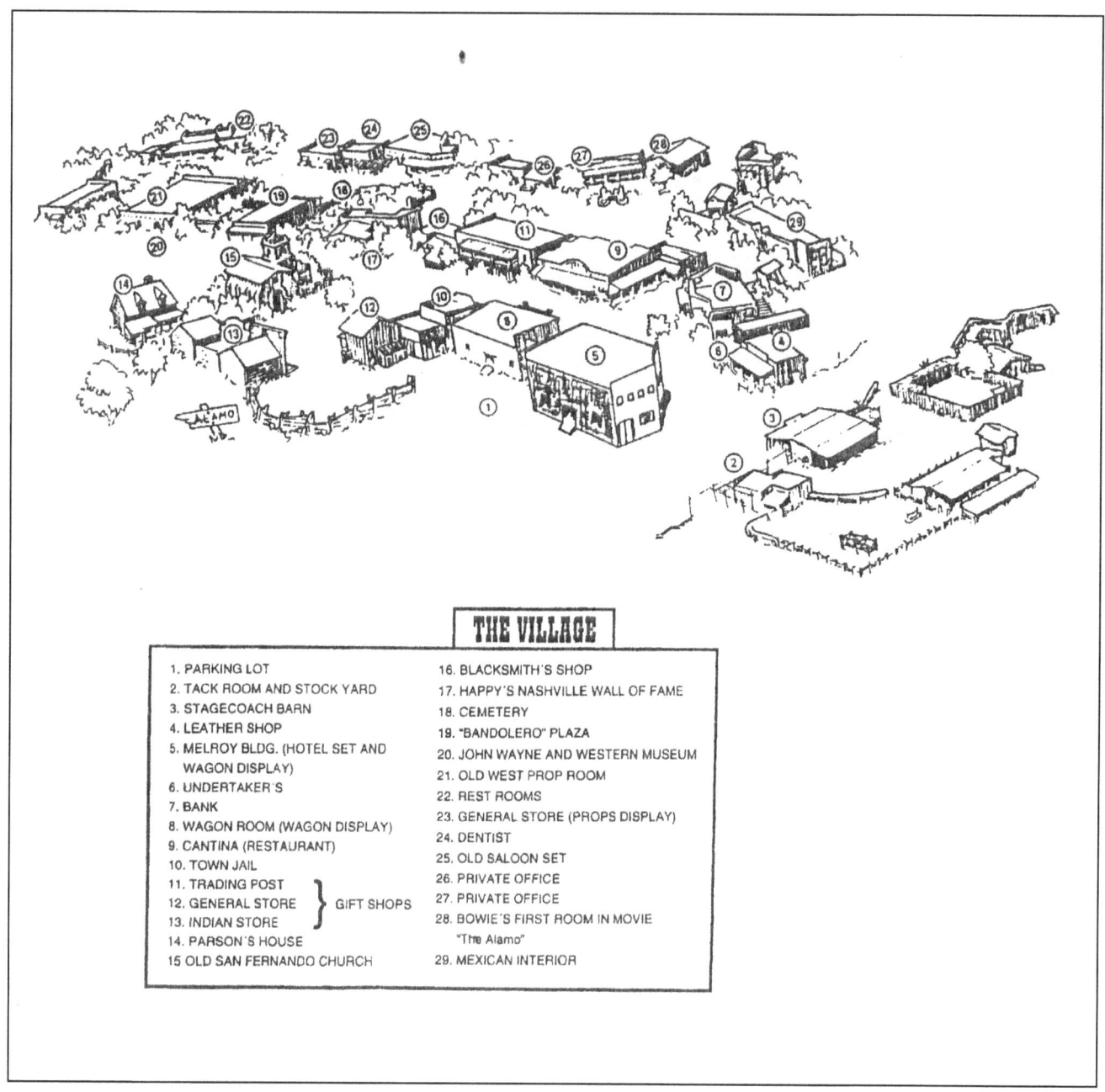

Alamo Village brochure, Alamo Village, c. 2001.

Just a cursory review of the Alamo Village grounds makes one question many of these "facts." For example, only two wells are currently present, not six: one on top of the hill "north" of the Alamo at the storage tank and another one in the Alamo Village cemetery. There may be one hundred or so trees and shrubs, but there aren't 5,000–that would be a veritable Garden of Eden. Only three buildings on the entire set had Spanish tile roofing: the San Fernando church, John Wayne's location office on Back Street and a building used for wardrobe storage on Front Street. That's an awful lot of tile for only three buildings. As Happy's entire ranch was only 22,000 acres, using 1,700 acres for stock corrals would take up almost 8 percent of the ranch. Probably not true; the entire Alamo compound, Village and corrals were more likely 400 acres. The landing strip looks to be about one thousand feet, not four thousand. In any case, exaggeration seemed to be modus operandi when publicizing the film.

Alamo Village was first and foremost a functioning working movie set and second, a western town entertainment park. As such, the architecture of the buildings and layout of the town changed depending upon the requirements of whatever film operation was present at the time. When first built, the Village consisted of nothing more than twenty buildings with two main "streets," creatively called Front Street and Back Street, dividing the town into fore and aft sections. (All names referred to are as they appear on the most recent Village brochure with the corresponding location number. *All italicized names identify the buildings as they appear in the film and/or on Ybarra's blueprints, along with appropriate Spanish signage.*) Along Front Street the buildings consisted of (2) the Tack Room (*House*), (3) Stagecoach Barn including the false adobe front behind it (*House*), (4) Leather Shop (*House*), (16) Blacksmith's Shop (*Blacksmith/Herrero, Warehouse/Almacenes, Coal Shed/Carboneria*), (17) Happy's Nashville Wall of Fame (*House*), (20) John and Wayne Western Museum, (21) Old West Prop Room (*Men's Wardrobe*), (9) Cantina, (11) Trading Post (*Hotel San Antonio*), and (7) Bank (*The Texan/El Texano, Hardware/Tlapaleria, Night Inn/Fonda Noche*). The un-numbered building between the (18) Cemetery and (19) "Bandolero" Plaza stored the *Women's Wardrobe*. The un-numbered building at the far end of Front Street opposite the Old West Prop Room was the *Make-up Bldg*. All the buildings along Front Street were on the same side of the street except for Old San Fernando Church. Lack of buildings on that side of the street would offer an unobstructed view from the Alamo to the town. Along Back Street, Ybarra's village consisted of (29) a Mexican Interior (the Veramendi Palace although at the time it just represented a typical Mexican building/*House*), a contiguous structure consisting of three businesses: (23) General Store, (24) Dentist Office, (25) Old Saloon Set (*My Small Cantina/Mi Cantinita, Passenger Hotel/Hosteria El Viajero*), (22) *Rest Rooms* (*Bakery/Panaderia/First Aid Room*), and a building housing (28) "Bowie's" room. Across the street from building (28) was another un-numbered building (*House*). On the opposite side of Front Street, The Old San Fernando Church (15) was constructed, including a gazebo and a low surrounding wall in front of the church.[75]

Everything was built so that it could be changed, modified, replaced or torn down if the need arose. The Village was almost complete from the church on down to the east side before construction began on the buildings to the west of the church. The church, as well as all of the rest of the buildings in the village, was constructed of adobe bricks. To accommodate door and windows salvaged from demolished buildings at Fort Clark ranch, specifically-sized openings were cut into the structures. The top portion of the bell tower of the San Fernando church (above the ledge) was built of wood and rigged to explode in an early version of the script. This was subsequently changed in later versions once Wayne agreed to Shahan's requirements for a loan. Climbing the stairs to the belfry, you will come to a wooden floor separating the tower from the building proper. The bell tower has four arched windows with shutters swinging inward, one in each geographic direction. The bell in the church tower was added for the TV movie *The Alamo: 13 Days to Glory* in 1986.[76]

Thatched-roof Mexican gazebo across Front Street from Hotel San Antonio looking southeast. Jacales and arched wall are seen in the distance at left and the Alamo compound at right. Reprinted with the permission of Richard Curilla/Alamo Village.

Initially identified as preliminary construction on the chapel and Long Barrack, this photograph in fact shows early work on the San Fernando church. The poles in the background pinpoint the eventual site of the Cantina. The vehicle at the top right edge of the photograph sits where the Stage Depot is now located on Front Street. Alamo Village Archives.

Preliminary construction of the Cantina and Hotel San Antonio on Front Street. The San Fernando Church, absent bell tower and belfry, can be seen on the left. Alamo Village Archives.

The San Fernando Church. Note all the vegetation in front of the church. This is the way the town looked before it was cleared and graded. Alamo Village Archives.

Further construction on Front Street. All buildings have been plastered and whitewashed, Hotel San Antonio now has a porch on its second level, and workmen are finishing the wrap-around roof on the Cantina. The bell tower also has been added to the San Fernando Church. Alamo Village Archives.

A beautiful photograph of San Fernando Church, c. 1960. This is almost exactly what the finished building looked like in "The Alamo" except for the addition of a contrasting accent strip around the light blue trim and the removal of the triangular caps on the ante-building posts. The scalloped wall was removed in September 1967 for "Bandolero!" The last building on the right, used as a make-up room for "The Alamo," had now been turned into an art studio for Bud Breen.

A close-up of Hotel San Antonio. The staircase leading to the second floor hasn't been added, nor have the shutters around the windows or signage. Trees and foliage would later be planted, including an oleander bush. Note that there isn't a door in the Cantina/Hotel wall directly behind the low wall to the right. An entrance hallway to the hotel stairs would later be added to accommodate a script change.

The completed Cantina and Hotel San Antonio as they appear in the film. A covered bank of 10 K carbon arc brute lights with night-blue for colored media stands on the roof of the hotel. They provided the soft blue base light for the moonlight scenes filmed in front of the hotel. Also note the window "flat" leaning against the wall on the far end of the hotel porch. This is the window through which Crockett looks into Flaca's room as she argues with Emil Sand.

As he stands on the roof of San Fernando Church, Alfred Ybarra inspects Front Street. Signage and set dressing are complete. From left to right, the buildings are: Almacenes/Warehouse, Herrero/Blacksmith, Hotel San Antonio, Cantina and Tlapaleria/Hardware.

The inside of the entrance to the Cantina as designed by Alfred Ybarra. Sadly, it was changed to a solid brick adobe wall with a doorway and windows within a year of filming. Reprinted with the permission of Richard Curilla/ Alamo Village.

A close-up of the vegetation in front of the hotel.

Front Street looking back toward San Fernando Church. The first building on the left housed the make-up department while men's wardrobe was stored in the next building up the street. Alamo Village Archives.

The next two photographs are panoramic views of San Antonio de Bexar. The village is now complete and in the first photo, you can see the remains of a four-arched wall and three jacales on the plain before the village. Trees line East Pinto Creek in the background.

In this photograph, you can see the hotel, church and numerous buildings on Back Street. This is the view the defenders would have if they stood on the cannon platform in the Alamo chapel. The large gap between the two buildings at the far left of Back Street is where the cattle were stampeded.

Reworking the script necessitated the completion of several adobe buildings on the street behind the Cantina as the layout of the set is always designed as a direct response to the needs of specific scenes. Some of the buildings would be finished in a way not readily apparent in the film, though, thus allowing them to be used as dressing rooms, medical facilities and commissary. They were also used to temporarily house the harnesses for caissons and bridles, saddles and reins. The use of individual buildings determined how they would be finished inside. On an early visit to the set, Wayne read the script and decided specific action should be moved around behind the main street—this required finishing several adobe structures. Peppered with names such as "Escuela para Ninos" (School for Children), "Huevos frescos" (Fresh eggs), and "Cantina," the village buildings served an entirely different but functional purpose. The Children's School was used as an air-conditioned make-up room, filled with dressing tables and brightly lighted mirrors. Wayne's office, the "Comanderia de Policia" or police station, with a red tile gabled roof located about halfway down Back Street, on the same side of the street as Bowie's room, had telecommunication capabilities and housed a plush lounge for the stars. The two-story Hotel San Antonio was a dining room for the cast and crew; the lower level filled with row after row of costume storage as was the Western Museum (men's) and the current Village general store (women's). After the film, Happy moved all the empty costume racks into the San Fernando Church where they remained until he installed pews from an old Brackettville church that was torn down. Also equipped with air-conditioning, the "Correo" (post office) was located next to the police station. (Wayne installed ten, three-ton A/C units in the mess and recreation halls, so cast and crew could relax in comfort, while the Mexican interior building (Veramendi Palace) housed an electrical generator.) The village included a hardware store (Tlapaleria), grocery store (Abarroles), pharmacy (Botica), coal shed (Carboneria), warehouse (Almacenes), bakery (Panaderia), two inns (Hosteria and Fonda Noche), barber shop (Barberia), and blacksmith shop (Herrero). During a tour of the village, Wayne told a reporter, "When we built these houses and decided to make them solid, we also made up our minds to make practical use of them. So we installed air-conditioning and moved in all our production departments. This way the prop section, costumes, makeup, the kitchen, and even the hospital are right where we are working. It saves us hours."[77]

The next series of photographs document Back Street. Houston and his troops are seen as they round the corner between the Cantina and the Tlapaleria building. This view is from the inside of a building identified as "Mexican Interior" on the current Alamo Village brochure. In the film, as Mexican lancers enter town, two young boys enter this building and close the window's shutters while a man places a large straw barrier in front of this opening. The Cantina's wrap-around roof is clearly visible as is the short roof over the rear entrance. Note the arched lattice window at the far right.

A partial rear view of the Cantina and Hotel San Antonio. Note the short blank wall that connects the two buildings. This will later be modified into a hallway and porch. The lower opening is a hallway from Front Street to Back.

John Wayne takes a break as he rides along Back Street. The Cantina's arched lattice window is now seen in its entirety; a porch and hallway have been added between the two buildings.

Individual restroom buildings for men and women also were constructed as was a medical first aid facility. Ybarra explained, "Around two thousand people will participate in the fighting. It's very likely some casualties will occur. Somebody usually gets hurt in falls from horses. Others get cut by bayonets, powder burns, etc." Two emergency rooms were set up to take care of the injuries. And a helicopter was also on hand to transport the seriously "wounded" to local hospitals. As for the restrooms, it was publicized that five miles of sewage lines were laid into massive leach fields. Three septic tanks were strategically located around the set; one behind the village restrooms, one behind Wayne's office, and one behind the Alamo compound restrooms. (Prior to the construction of Duke's office in the village, whenever he was checking on construction, Wayne would stay at Happy's ranch in what was known as the "White house," the original Webb family residence.)[78]

Grant was effusive in his praise of Ybarra's efforts; "This set is tremendous, just great. There is no cheating here—no false fronts or painted backgrounds—but you don't need anything in this area. This is the greatest area for movies I've seen. You can find everything here: sand dunes, real rough country, timbered areas, and that sky. I've never seen such a perfect sky in my life. This area is definitely bound to figure in more movies. It has a terrific potential." Stunt coordinator Cliff Lyons called it the "most fantastic set I've seen in twenty-five years in the movies. If you pull

The evacuation of San Antonio. Wayne is standing on the small porch identified in the previous photograph. The building at the far right is Bowie's room where Jethro and his master discuss Houston's departure and Bowie's ailment. The next building to the left of the cemetery is the Comanderia de Policia/Police Station/Wayne's Batjac office. Its window air-conditioning unit was painted green in an unsuccessful attempt to camouflage it.

A workman applies texture to the "shrine" as Ybarra called it on his blueprint. Wayne's Batjac office is being built at the left. This became a corner structure of a fenced-in goat yard where building 27 now stands.

Looking east out the rear gate from Back Street. Houston's departing troops passed right to left across the front of the building on the left and continued on the road to East Pinto Creek. Reprinted with the permission of Richard Curilla/Alamo Village.

The far west end of Back Street. The current village restrooms are in the center of the photograph; a small cantina is on the right. Alamo Village Archives.

A workman patches a pillar on the corner of the Campo Santo further down Back Street behind the cemetery while another workman applies texture to it.

Looking northwest across Back Street from the second-story Cantina back porch at a jacal and rear gate. Reprinted with the permission of Richard Curilla/Alamo Village.

A view of San Fernando Church and the Carroceria taken from under a porch in front of the Passenger Inn.

Back Street looking southwest from behind the Cemetery. Cattle, stampeded between the tree and the building on the right, then turned left and headed down the street. Two frightened Mexican soldados leapt over the scalloped wall seen in the previous photograph. Reprinted with the permission of Richard Curilla/ Alamo Village.

A wrangler works with a horse in one of the many corrals constructed on Shahan's ranch.

out all the cameras and cables and dumped some movie men in here, they'd never believe it was a movie set. It's just too real. I've never seen anything like this street. There's no worrying about angles; you just shoot every side of it. There's no doubt this area has a big future waiting. I told Duke, 'Duke, if you don't take advantage of this and make another movie here real quick, you're really missing out.'" Publicist Henaghan, as usual, went a bit overboard: "The entire town has been constructed to scale. When we are through, we'll leave it to Mr. Shahan. What else can we do with it? But first we're going to blow the dickens out of it." Wayne may have had an ulterior motive when he decided to take that approach. Reportedly, he was unhappy it would be used for television shows after his film was complete and one way to prevent that was to destroy the set. Just as Wayne played a bit fast and loose with factual accuracy and the chapel, so did Henaghan when it came to the village: "It is a practical livable set," he stated. "Six or seven thousand people could live there." Well, with only nineteen buildings in the village, that would equate to a minimum of three hundred inhabitants in each structure. With a set rumored to cost between $500,000 and $1,500,000 to construct, Wayne had to spend $70,000 to revamp some of the quarters at Fort Clark where cast and crew were staying, which made Batjac's tight-fisted comptroller Al Podlasky none-too-happy.[79]

Wayne was more than satisfied as he performed a final walk through the set. All buildings aged effectively, props and set dressing staged correctly. Authentic adobe blocks were used for the walls and buildings—no false fronts for Duke. It was as if he had been transported back to 1836 San Antonio. As he walked with his entourage through the compound, he stopped momentarily and studied the chapel. Something wasn't right. Suddenly, it came to him. Ybarra had placed a small white cross on top of the parapet. "Take that down," he ordered. A construction worker immediately did so. Duke paused, and then gave Ybarra direction. "That was Wayne's idea," said Al. "We were looking at the set with the cameraman and he said, 'Gimme something on top of the set. Something allegorical.' His exact words. He said, 'Get a cross up there.' I said, 'No problem.' And put a cross up there. The thing didn't belong. It was all out of scale and everything. No one could say it wasn't there originally. No one knew and no one cared. So I put it up there. Fortunately I put a platform up on top of the Alamo just in case there was some action he might require that was not in the script. I got it, reinforced it, and finally shot some action up there."

The cross, built out of a shipping pallet and placed at an angle to represent a fallen cross, was attached to a stand, so it could be positioned correctly. Two cannons were placed on the gun platform; a small one just beneath the cross and a larger one pointing toward the town. Photos suggest the cross was braced against the back of the Alamo "hump" by the cedar gun platform. The subsequent larger cross gave the chapel the necessary character needed and was just what Wayne was looking for. Ybarra admitted, "Duke had a very good eye for small details like that—for film composition—he has never been recognized for that."[80]

An aerial view of San Antonio de Bexar, c. 1959.

An aerial view of Alamo Village, c. Summer 1966. The Tascosa two-story hotel for "Two Rode Together" has been added to Front Street; the cemetery on Back Street between Bowie's room and Wayne's headquarters building has been replaced by a building later used as a photo gallery.

The following series of photographs display the now almost-ready Alamo compound. The rear of the Alamo chapel can be seen with limestone rubble still piled in front of the church, indicating that the facade is not yet complete, the palisade is missing, the courtyard behind the Long Barrack is yet to be finished as is its ramada, and the chapel parapet. Although plastered and whitewashed, the buildings still needed to be textured and aged. A tank/pond is visible outside the West Wall in front of "Smitty's Hill." According to Ybarra's original blueprints, the Convento courtyard rear wall and gate were deliberately omitted. It was only after the script was changed that the courtyard walls were moved and expanded. Alamo Village Archives. 2300-05.

An aerial view of the Alamo compound; adobe bricks are drying in front of the South Wall; the village of San Antonio de Bexar can be seen in the upper right corner of the photograph.

A view of the southwest corner of the compound. An electrical power pole is in front of the flagpole mound; the small white cross on the chapel parapet has not yet been replaced.

The Alamo chapel is now finished, including iconic "fallen" cross and cannon. The façade is complete, the building aged and textured.

The Alamo compound as seen in the film: the mound has a flagpole on it, the cattle corral is up, the courtyard is finished, the palisade is in place. Three jacales and a four-arched wall can be seen on the plain between the set and the village.

The ruins of Travis's headquarters (note fireplace on second-story right wall) and the Alamo church. This was taken from the flagpole mound in the middle of the plaza. Virtually the entire second floor of the headquarters building was destroyed, including the porch, roof and staircase. Reprinted with the permission of Richard Curilla/Alamo Village.

The north side of the Alamo chapel with the breach through which Mexican soldiers attacked Jim Bowie. Reprinted with the permission of Richard Curilla/Alamo Village.

Wall connecting the Long Barrack with the Alamo chapel. Happy's new plaster (here with just first coat) over Wayne's bare adobe brick would protect the sets by keeping the mud-adobe from washing away. He also whitewashed the plaster after the second coat was applied to make it impervious to rain. Reprinted with the permission of Richard Curilla/Alamo Village.

At the conclusion of filming of *The Alamo*, the set was in pretty bad shape. The West Wall was partially demolished from the southwest corner going "north" all along its length to a point directly across from the middle of the Long Barrack. This would have included Bowie's quarters, which were about two hundred feet from the southwest cannon ramp. Demolition was deliberate–the space allowed Wayne to film the panoramic final scene with the Alamo chapel in the background as Susanna, her daughter Lisa and Happy Sam leave the ruins, passing Santa Anna on their way out. (Jose Hernandez, the young son of "Chato" Hernandez, was originally asked to be in this scene, leading the donkey that John Wayne's young daughter Aissa sat on. The Hernandez family decided it would be too dangerous and turned down the offer. Instead, nine-year-old John Henry Daniels of Brackettville was chosen. John Henry's brother Caesar also had a part in the movie.) A portion of the north wall of the side room in the north transept area was blasted out as well. Wayne's tree near the collapse of the North Wall was blackened from fire and the breach in the wall was apparent. The top ridge of the West Wall consisted of scorched jagged holes in an irregular pattern as a result of Mexican artillery explosions as did the upper and lower portion of the Long Barrack. The upper portion of Travis's headquarters was completely demolished with only the northern and southern walls still standing. The floor's burnt timbers were still in place while the fireplace clung to the second-story wall with no visible means of support. Scorch marks singed the walls of the chapel and compound. The cannons were still there, parked in rows with limbers and caissons outside the wall. Broken rifles, bayonets, and lockplates were scattered across the plain, along with ladders and other props. Styrofoam rocks and pieces of walls were lying about, and one visitor reported finding a flat piece of Styrofoam in the shape of a human head—no doubt the remnants of a stunt gag. All in all, the compound was devastated.[81]

Wayne walks across the devastated Alamo plaza in preparation for the final non-combatant departure scene. Taken from the roof over the Main Gate, the second floor of Travis's headquarters is demolished. Note scorch marks on various buildings around the compound.

Virginia Shahan in the rear courtyard behind the Long Barrack. The ramada has partially collapsed. Reprinted with the permission of Richard Curilla/Alamo Village.

The flagpole mound where Crockett unhorsed a Mexican trooper was still there however, as was the corral, but the mound was eventually leveled and the material used to provide adobe blocks for the jail in *Bandolero!* The chapel's southern-most wall was partially destroyed as a result of the explosion in the powder magazine. The southern transept of the chapel was also demolished so that Carlos Arruza could ride into the area where Mrs. Dickinson and the two children were discovered. The perspective of that particular scene was filmed from the point of view of Mrs. Dickinson. She was hiding with the children in the far northeast corner of the apse. Also, Parson's death scene was filmed in a spot directly opposite the southeast corner of the southern transept. Some portions of the set destroyed during filming were later reconstructed using lathe, plaster and wood. It cost Happy almost $50,000 to bring the set back to a presentable condition. Most damaged portions were just re-plastered and whitewashed.[82]

Another view of the Convento courtyard behind the Long Barrack. You can also see the remains of Travis's headquarters; obviously some of the destruction debris has already been removed.

Looking through the utility entrance to the Alamo compound at the ruins of the West Wall and cedar post ramada. Notice that a first coat of plaster has already been applied to the end of the Long Barrack adobe at the upper left. The current restrooms are directly behind you. Reprinted with the permission of Richard Curilla/Alamo Village.

The northern end of the Long Barrack. Scorch marks from numerous explosions are readily apparent.

Northeast corner of the Alamo compound. Once again, one can see scorch marks on the ruined buildings. The flaming tree that Mexican Dragoons rode past by as they entered the compound is in the center of the photo.

Two jornos and a collapsed ramada along the ruined West Wall.

The Alamo compound as viewed from the North Wall. Notice the squared-off top to the Main Gate. This photograph was taken after the completion of "Two Rode Together" in 1960.

For those interested in the location of where specific scenes were filmed, the following are offered:

1. Ybarra created a ten-foot-tall, southwest corner of the Alamo chapel façade replica, about a half mile to the east of the main set, including cannon platform and portable fallen cross. It is still on-site to this day, albeit without a cannon, platform or cross. This structure was used for all close-up scenes involving Wayne, Widmark, and Harvey atop the platform. One way to determine exactly where a scene atop the chapel was filmed is to look at the

Wayne, Harvey, Widmark et al. atop the faux Alamo. Note the apple box that Harvey is standing on. The cannon is also braced with two-by-fours, with gas canisters connected to the cannon to simulate a discharge.

An interior view of the faux chapel. The platform and cannon have long since been removed, c. 2013.

angle of the camera. If you can see the whole Alamo building from a distance, it was filmed on the main set. If the camera looks up at or is level with the platform and you only see a close-up of the top of the chapel, it was probably filmed off-site. As you stand behind the fake wall and face outward, much as Travis did when he fired the cannon at Santa Anna, the caliche pit and the field between this set and the main compound are directly behind you. A copy of the "allegorical" cross was built on a moveable platform or tripod, and used in a variety of shots. You also can tell which site was used by looking at the cross. Apparently, the two crosses weren't identical in size. An analysis of still photos taken during filming reveals that the upper cross-member of the faux-top cross is longer in length than the one atop the main set. The latter cross also was directly attached to the back of the parapet of the chapel while the cross on the moveable platform/tripod appears to be slightly offset from the back of the wall. The route to this location is marked by a winding, rutted, rock-strewn, almost impassible dirt road but it is not on the Alamo Village grounds proper and cannot be visited without the permission and presence of a guide.

2. Two interior sets were created on a makeshift sound stage in the old corrugated metal airplane hangar located in the far southwestern corner of the Fort Clark Guest Ranch property: a lobby that represented Travis's headquarters in San Antonio, and a hallway, vestibule, and hotel room from the Hotel San Antonio for Flaca. At seventy-five feet by one hundred twenty, the building, said to be the second-oldest hangar in the country, was not terribly large but big enough to accommodate cast, crew, various walls, lights, etc. Cheaper than paying outrageous studio rental fees, it was convenient, functional, and available. While Wayne was busy filming the opening scene the previous day, his gaffers, grips, electricians, carpenters, and other assorted tradesmen were constructing interior sets. Unfortunately, it wasn't air-conditioned. Heavy wooden beams simulated a room's ceiling structure but also supported overhead lighting and technicians. Mounted on wooden scaffolding, these lights poured out tremendous heat; fans and air-conditioners couldn't be used—their noise could be picked up by microphones. The hangar doors were closed to muffle outside sounds. The non-air-conditioned sets were constructed by using numerous "walls" in a variety of configurations; thus they were able to use the hangar as a sound stage. In all probability, the sets were constructed facing each other across the hangar, so the same lighting equipment could be used for both with a minimum of re-rigging. As both sets were three-sided with no parallel walls, elements such as a window were placed in the foreground to create depth. The hotel lobby was located on one of the long sides of the hangar and Flaca's room on the other. The floor of the hangar was a poured concrete pad; one can clearly see its expansion joints in the scenes filmed at this location.

A DC-3 parked in front of Fort Clark hangar built in 1921, the second-oldest hangar in the country behind Randolph Air Force base in San Antonio. The sign over the open doors reads "Fort Clark Field." Reprinted with the permission of William Haenn/Warren Studio, Del Rio, Texas.

A current photograph of the Fort Clark hangar, c. 2006. Broken window panes and overgrown trees frame the hangar.

Scene 21, take 4. Officers call, Fort Clark hangar soundstage. Lights are suspended between the large timber beams and roof. Left to right: unknown extra, Joseph Calleia (seated), Julian Trevino, Richard Boone, Bill Daniel, Laurence Harvey, Pat Wayne, Ken Curtis and Bill Henry.

John Wayne waits patiently for his cue as Wesley Lau reads his lines to Linda Cristal. Flaca's room was the second set constructed on the hangar soundstage.

3. During the Raid for Cattle sequence, Travis and numerous defenders hold off pursuing Mexican dragoons from behind a cedar-post fence connected to three jacales by a four-arch adobe wall. This fence was located at an angle (about one hundred fifty yards away from the South Wall) on the right side of a dirt road, halfway between the Alamo and the village. After filming ended, the outworks were still present although in a somewhat battered shape. Today, all that remains are three mounds of caliche, scattered stones from the ruined adobe walls and a jorno (outdoor oven) standing next to a gnarled, prickly tree. During filming, additional jornos were placed inside the compound– under a ramada along the West Wall and in front of the horse corral facing the North Wall.

The lone remaining jorno on the Alamo set, located on the plain between the Alamo set and the village, c. 2006.

4. Across from the Fort Clark golf course pro shop and four hundred yards upstream along the banks of Las Moras Creek is the spot where Houston's camp was situated. As you face the pro shop across the creek, and immediately before you cross the small cart bridge, look to your left down the narrow road that runs parallel to the creek. If you go down the road about two hundred feet, an adobe wall ruin is on your left. Although constructed for Wayne's movie, it wasn't used in any scenes. It can be seen, however, in *Two Rode Together*. As dimwits Greeley and Ortho Cleeg (Ken Curtis and Harry Carey, Jr.) comically attack defenseless First Lt. Jim Gary (Richard Widmark), a drunken Marshal Guthrie McCabe (James Stewart) offers constructive criticism: "*Foul, Jim. Foul.*" Stewart is hunkered down in front of this wall. The creek to your right where Andy Devine uses his belly to bump both Cleggs into the water is where Houston's camp was located. A visual reconciliation of the current landscape with the filmed scenes verifies this conclusion as well as a then-and-now photo comparison. To be honest, though, there is some question whether the Houston campsite scene was filmed at Fort Clark or eighty miles away along the banks of the Sabinal River. Selective recall and age all seems to color our memories. There are those who are absolutely adamant that certain scenes were filmed in particular areas while others' memories equally convince them otherwise. Local Sabinal residents are positive that not only were the camp scenes filmed there, but Richard Boone was definitely present

Carlos Arruza and his Mexican lancers ride past an arched adobe wall constructed by Chato Hernandez.

as well. Along with the presence of large numbers of extras and horsemen, some even recall making lunch for the various actors. Others are positive in their disagreement and state that it had to be Fort Clark. After comparing all accounts and visual information, it is clear that the Houston headquarter tent scene was filmed at Fort Clark. Through the magic of movies, seamless splicing of the two sequences gives the appearance of a continuous scene filmed at the same location.[83]

The remains of the arched wall, directly across the road from Houston's campsite on Las Moras Creek, c. 2006.

Houston's camp site on the banks of Las Moras Creek, c. 2006.

5. As Crockett and his Tennesseans approach the outskirts of San Antonio, they traverse a lush, grassy flatland with rousting quail and bounding deer. Juan Seguin, his son and bodyguard are later seen riding through this same field on their way to the Alamo to report details of Santa Anna's advance. These two scenes, along with the scene where Santa Anna's army advances over mountain and plain, were all filmed on Bill Moody's old Leona ranch, located roughly six to eight miles north of Alamo Village.[84]

6. The "Flaca's tree" sequence was filmed on the banks of the Sabinal River, eight miles below Utopia and one hundred yards from the highway bridge, on the old McCullough ranch, eighty miles from Brackettville: *"There's right and there's wrong—you gotta do one or the other. You do the one and you're living. You do the other, and you may be walking around, but you're as dead as a beaver hat."* A magnificent setting complete with wide stream, large picturesque cypress trees, and tall bluffs provided a colorful background. The property was perfect for Wayne's requirements, and, as a result, several scenes were filmed there: the aforementioned tree scene, Smitty's crossing of a stream with waterfall and subsequent meeting a sentry outpost (*"Corporal of the guard, post number three!"*), his approach to the outskirts of Houston's camp, and the morning patrol/cattle sequence that was subsequently cut. Microphones, holders and sound equipment remained in Flaca's tree when the crew returned to Brackettville and to create an easement so horses could cross, truckloads of stones were poured into the stream downriver from the dam. After this scene was finished, the owner of the property had to pay for a bulldozer to remove the stones. Sadly, the magnificent cypress tree Wayne and Cristal stood under is no longer there as it was washed away in a 1986 flood. It was said the water rose so high lawn furniture was discovered in upper tree limbs.[85]

A small waterfall on the Sabinal River property of Crystal Harvey Wade. In order to capture this view, Frankie Avalon rode from left to right across this river as we look upstream, c. 2008.

The Sabinal River, complete with large bluffs and magnificent cypress trees. Frankie Avalon again rode left to right in this view looking downstream, basically retracing his steps! Once he reached the river's bank he met Houston's sentries ("Corporal of the guard, post number three!")

Flaca's tree. "Lord above! That's one beautiful tree! This tree must've been growed before man put his first dirty footprints on this prairie. Kind of a tree Adam and Eve must have met under. You know something, Flaca? I guess I saw a who-knows-how-many trees before I ever took a long, thoughtful look at one. Mostly I looked at a tree to see was there a bear in it or an Indian behind it."

7. At the beginning of the movie, immediately after Houston's confrontation with Travis during officers' call, Houston leaves the hotel and meets Bowie's servant Jethro, directly in front of a large tree. Brackettville resident Chuck Hall vividly recalls this scene: Dressed in a long-sleeve shirt, dark pants, boots and slouch hat, the youngster stands next to a woman and little girl as Boone walks by to speak with Hairston. Seven seconds later, though, in an over-the-shoulder shot of Boone and Hairston, Chuck now is sitting in the crook of a tree, immediately behind Hairston. "Wayne placed me in that tree," says Hall. "He did that personally." This scene was filmed on Back Street, directly behind The Trading Post (11). After a brief conversation, Jethro appears to walk into the doorway in the back of a building (16) where a drunk, sleeping Bowie lies. However, the interior of this room was, in fact, shot across the street in building 28. Due to the skillful talent of the film's editor, no one was the wiser.[86]

8. The scene where runway Mexican artillery caissons rush across a creek in chaotic fashion was filmed on the L.L. Davis ranch along the banks of the West Nueces River next door to Moody's ranch. The dry riverbed is much as it was when the movie was filmed, though now overgrown with trees, shrubs and scrub. A remote-controlled Mitchell camera was positioned on a grip-flat in the middle of the stream so that its lens was slightly above water level. The horses were supposed to "split the camera," alternating on either side. Artillerymen are seen roaring down Old Silver Lake Road at full gallop with caissons in tow. In front were two riders leading four horses pulling a limber attached to a cannon. Quickly, the team made a sharp right turn, headed down the bank of the stream and galloped across. One, two, three teams successfully negotiated the stunt although one rider was bucked

Left to right: Richard Boone, Chuck Hall, Jester Hairston, Marshall Jones (Wayne's lighting stand-in). As this scene finishes, Hairston enters the doorway on the far left of the photograph but…

...he actually enters the building across the street that was used as the interior of Bowie's room. A current view shows that it is only slightly different from its appearance in the film, however the breach/window on the left wall has been totally bricked in, c. 2014

off one horse and landed on another. One caisson broke loose as the team rounded the turn and started to slide down the bank; the out-of-control horses split and ran over the camera. After the camera flipped and settled upside down at the bottom of the stream, a technician ran into the shallow water, and tried to salvage it. Though submerged, the camera was still running. When the film magazine was unloaded it was found that it was still in perfect condition. The result was a memorable scene that was the result of a fortunate accident. (The scene where Mexican dragoons cross a stream in front of several impressive bluffs was filmed in the same general area about two hundred yards downstream along the Tularosa road.)[87]

9. A scene filmed at Las Moras Creek on the Ft Clark reservation showed Mexican soldiers being pulled backward over the railing of a road bridge. The trestle bridge's superstructure, including deck, railings and support members, was held up by timber beams. The deck was covered with ten two by twelve inch wooden planks placed edge to edge across its width. It appears that the three-board upstream railing had its center board removed to allow easy

An artillery caisson races toward the river bank, immediately followed by a second unit. Other caissons are staged on Old Silver Lake Road at the far left.

The camera platform lies smashed in the middle of the stream while a second caisson veers to avoid it. Other caisson units have been held because of the accident.

A gravel and stock crossing over the West Nueces River where the scene was filmed. Now, it's just a dry riverbed, c. 2014.

Later that same day, Mexican dragoons were filmed riding down the West Nueces while several peasants watch their advance. This scene was filmed several times–a few riders had a tendency to fall off their horses. Notice the bluffs in the left background.

access for stuntmen as they climbed over the railing. The Tennesseans' final rush to the bridge was filmed on the upstream side of the bridge, with the camera position on the same side of the bank under a large tree. This was done to provide a more picturesque shot of the bridge. Since the screen left-to-right movement was preserved, it didn't matter that the Tennesseans were actually walking downstream instead of upstream. The original bridge superstructure has long since been dismantled but the old original footings can still be seen next to the new bridge. The U.S. Army had built the road bridge many years earlier. To see this site, enter the Fort Clark main gate, cross the bridge and continue until you reach the first stop sign. Turn left and drive toward the Museum and Stables. (Built ca. 1870 and used by the cavalry for the headquarters troop, the stables are presently used by the Fort Clark Springs Horse Club.) At the end of this road, you will reach a small parking area on

The bluffs, c. 2014.

    the right-hand side of the road. Park your vehicle and walk about thirty yards toward the creek. Directly in front of you will be the new footbridge.[88]

10. About forty yards from that site, to your right on the same side of the river, just downstream from the bridge, is the area where the Flamenco dance scene was filmed. Recently cleared of secondary growth, a portion of the original structure still remains. Chato Hernandez had built an adobe wall to replicate one seen in John Singer Sargent's famous 1882 painting *El Jaleo*. In fact, Duke had a copy of the print on-site to assure complete accuracy of prop placement and set dressing. Although staged in front of the wall, the Flamenco scene was

The current footbridge over Las Moras Creek, c. 2014. The Tennesseans' final rush to the bridge was filmed from the upstream side of the bridge under this tree. Although it appears in the film that the two Mexican sentries are stationed on the right-hand end of this bridge, in fact, that portion of the scene was filmed on the left-hand end. The creek was dammed to increase the depth of the water.

filmed from the opposite bank as Crockett and his volunteers wade downstream from screen left to screen right in the foreground. It is interesting to note that this scene was filmed at night and it was so foggy that wind machines were used to dispel enough of the fog so that the actors could be seen.[89]

11. Three "tanks," or ponds, are located on Shahan's property just across the road from the West Wall of the Alamo compound set. They were man-made and the dirt road from the gate in the West Wall that leads to the faux Alamo top crosses between two of them. The pond on the right shows up in the scene where wounded Mexican soldiers from the first assault walk along its far bank. The second production unit, directed by Michael Wayne, filmed this scene. This pond is the first of three ponds across from the West Wall looking back toward the wall. In fact, if the camera's viewpoint had been slightly elevated, you would've seen the West Wall. This tank appears again when Susanna Dickenson walks out in the final scene up the far hill where she meets Smitty. A third tank was located just to the east of the jacales mentioned in item #3.

John Singer Sargent's 1882 painting, El Jaleo (The Ruckus). Wayne had a copy of the painting on hand to assure that his staging of the dance scene exactly duplicated the poses.

The scene as filmed. Note that the positioning of the various individuals, the placement of the set dressing and even the color of the costumes are an exact replication of Sargent's painting. Wayne, Widmark and Chill Wills can be seen in the creek, slowly emerging from the mist.

The remains of the wall Chato Hernandez built for this scene, c. 2005. Prior to the clearing of the area, this site was almost inaccessible.

A view of the location from across the creek, c. 2005. This is the position the camera was in as the scene was filmed. All that remains of the large tree under which the Tennesseans pass is the small object in the center of the photograph.

The lone survivors. John Henry Daniels leads the jenny "Maria" past one of the tanks outside the West Wall. The ruined Alamo can clearly be seen in the background. Wayne's young daughter Aissa sits astride the mule as Joan O'Brien holds her in place. Filmed in several segments, sharp-eyed observers will notice the size of the dirt smudge on Aissa's face increases as she rides along.

Overgrown trees now line this tank's bank, c. 2014. The Main Gate and Alamo chapel are visible between the trees. This tank is the one closest to the village. Happy built earthen dams across the dry run-off stream that comes down from the small canyon between Parson's Hill and Smitty's Hill. After a few days of rain, these three tanks were full of water.

12. Not everyone realizes that there isn't a basement under the San Fernando church, and it appears the night scene in the *basement* actually *may* have been filmed during the day. Clothier had the grip department build a twelve by twelve foot wooden enclosure as an extension of the church for camera and crew. The large double doors on the back of the low part of the church were removed like a "wild wall" to let the camera and crew set up outside the basement area seen in the film. Blackout tarps to keep out exterior sunlight enclosed the plywood room, front church window, and doorway. Small doorways to the outside on the front and side walls of the low building were covered with adobe bricks to simulate the look of buttresses in an underground basement. The staircase to the bell tower doubled as stairs to the basement. Lit with movie lights for a torchlight effect, the set could now be used during the day as day-for-night without going into a more expensive nighttime schedule.[90]

Davy Crockett, Jim Bowie and Emil Sand at the foot of the "basement" stairs. "Is… is he dead?" "Well, sort of."

The enclosed plywood room outside the church. Reprinted with the permission of Richard Curilla/Alamo Village.

A variety of scenes were filmed in and around the hills and valleys surrounding the main set.[91]

13. Immediately following the scene in which Travis fires a cannon in response to Santa Anna's demands, Mexican troops are shown marching along the ridge of a hill. As you drive down the road toward the Alamo compound, look to the left at Parson's Hill just before you reach the beginning of the West Wall. That's the same camera angle that was used for the Mexican column. "Parson's Hill" is the name given to that mount where Parson and Smitty first gaze upon San Antonio.

14. The Mexican camp in the cattle-stealing and European cannon scenes was filmed in the same general area. The camp was set up north of the eastern end of the Village, with East Pinto Creek as a backdrop. The European cannon scene was filmed in the creek bed a quarter mile from this spot, in front of the Alamo.

15. A portion of the cattle stampede was filmed about nine hundred yards from the village near the airstrip. With wranglers dressed as buckskinned defenders interspersed among the actors and stuntmen, a camera truck raced along the airstrip while the cattle were driven beside it in a running shot. Once this shot was complete, the cattle were herded behind the village set on the far side of Pinto Creek. Wayne, as Crockett, yelled "Let's take 'em," and the cattle began to run across the plain between Pinto Creek and the scenery flats. Although it appears as a continuous sequence (a product of carefully planned direction of movement

Alamo defenders stampede cattle through the Mexican camp. According to one extra, Duke unsuccessfully tried several times to run the cattle through the camp (he had difficulty with the extras not staying in their proper places). Not satisfied with the results, the cattle were then stampeded down Back Street.

on the screen), the remaining portions of the cattle stampede were filmed as four separate actions. In each, the cattle were re-grouped and then moved in the appropriate direction, according to the screen direction plan. In the first action, the cattle were driven right to left on the far side of Pinto Creek. After the cameras and necessary equipment were placed in the next position (across the creek behind the village), the cattle were re-staged, then filmed as they moved across the dammed-up creek to the right of the bathrooms on Back Street in the Village as you look toward them. Then those set-ups were struck and moved into the village for further angles of the stampede through Back Street. The cattle then were regrouped in the pasture beyond the left end of the village and held until the action call. In the last action, the herd ran down the length of Back Street and turned toward the Alamo. The "haciendas" seen on the opposite side of East Pinto Creek are, in fact, scenery "flats," large screen elements on plaster-covered fiberboard. Painted with doors and windows to look like outlying buildings, they served to make the film's "San Antonio" look larger than it actually was. You can also see the front side of these "flats" in the scene where Parson and Smitty first see San Antonio. They serve to extend the village length to both the right and left. If you own the widescreen version of the movie, in one shot you can see the left flats next to Smitty's head and the right flats in the cloud shadow beyond the village on the right

Cattle stampede across East Pinto Creek behind the village.

side of the frame. Always in "deep background," they're about two hundred to three hundred yards out in the brush across Pinto Creek and virtually inaccessible. Alas, all that remains are iron end-post pipes and white and light-blue plaster.[92]

16. In an extended sequence, several scouts, chased by Mexican dragoons, ride hell-bent-for-leather into the Alamo compound. Directed by stunt coordinator Cliff Lyons, Rudy Robbins, Big Boy Williams, and two other defenders discover the "European cannon" and ride back to the Alamo to notify the garrison. "As you are coming (on to the set) and you pass the horse corrals on the right," recalled Robbins, "there is a ranch road, mostly grown over by now, that continues on due east from where the corrals are. It goes back a mile or two on the ranch to an old house and a set of ranch working pens. This road was kept well graded at the time of the filming, and the airstrip was on the south side of this road, about a half mile east of the Alamo. Because of this well-graded road, several of the movie scenes were filmed out that way, as it was an easy area to get to. Most of the ranch was grown over in brush, and hard to access. This is the same area where me and Big Boy and the other scouts were when the Mexicans got after us, and we made a dash for the Alamo."[93]

17. Before the final battle, Santa Anna and his staff are seen trotting toward the top of a hill. This was filmed on the hill directly in front of the Alamo, looking southeast, opposite the West Wall. In the distance, you can plainly see Pinto Creek, bordered by trees. This hill is also where Santa Anna viewed the battle and where Smitty meets Mrs. Dickinson in the final scene.

18. Though not a part of the movie set per se, the Palisado, located at Fort Clark, has a tangential connection to the film. During preproduction, Batjac funds were used to renovate numerous buildings at Fort Clark to house both cast and crew. Given the resort's age and run-down condition, restoration was equally welcome and necessary. All buildings were not refurbished, however, with many left in a state of disrepair. Since John Ford and Jack Pennick previously had served in the military and naturally were interested in the area's history, both spent one late-September Sunday exploring the fort's grounds. The pair eventually came upon a vertical log-constructed, cedar post structure the fort's civilian owners identified as the Robert E. Lee Courthouse. Saddened by its neglect but impressed by its former occupant, Ford spoke to several cast and crewmembers later that evening and all agreed to restore the building. As a result, six men, including Pennick, Ernie Saftig, and Hank Worden, spent their next five Sundays repairing the structure's interior and exterior: broken windows, doors, furniture, etc. The surrounding grounds also were spruced up with a rail fence and gravel pathway. Once finished, the final touch was to add a commemorative white two-foot by four-foot sign constructed by the Batjac paint shop. Two wooden one-foot by two-foot flags were attached: an 1860 United States flag and a Confederate "Stars and Bars." On the sign, it simply read *"Robert E. Lee, Lt. Colonel U.S.A. Last Post Of Command."(A touching tribute, unfortunately misdirected. The refurbished building in fact was "The Palisado Building Kitchen/Messroom." Constructed in 1869-70 by the Buffalo Soldiers of the Twenty-fifth Infantry, it eventually also served as a company storeroom, tailor shop, and amusement hall. Robert E. Lee never visited Fort Clark, and the building wasn't constructed until eight years after he'd left Texas.)*[94]

Commended for their efforts but misinformed in their endeavor, Jack Pennick and production assistant Ernie Saftig view their tribute to Robert E. Lee.

The Palisado, c. 2014.

John Ford aka "Pappy," "Jack," or "Coach," prepares to direct a scene.

19. In addition to the Palisado, Fort Clark's post headquarters also was *involved* in the film, albeit not seen on screen. Built in 1857, the structure originally had served as the commanding officer's quarters and then post headquarters. Following World War I, the building was expanded, doubling its size with additional office space and a second story added by 1943. The building faced the fort's original parade grounds and sat adjacent to the Duplex Officer's Quarters (Officer's Mess and Club) and Post Theater. Then serving as Batjac's administrative headquarters, and providing temporary housing for members of the cast and crew, the building caught fire during the afternoon of November 15, 1959. Payroll, accounting, and casting departments were on the first floor and assistant director Robert Relyea had a room on the second floor along with two second assistants and several script clerks. Glen Tetens, Fort Clark manager, reported the fire began on the second floor and estimated damage at $75,000. It was believed the fire may have been started due to an oil furnace malfunction or faulty kerosene heater. The remains of the abandoned structure can still be seen today, sadly empty and in disrepair.[95]

Fort Clark Ranch Headquarters, c. 1950s.

The November 15 fire at Fort Clark. Members of the Brackettville, Del Rio, and Laughlin Air Force Base fire departments rush to put out the blaze to no avail. Even actors Ken Curtis and John Dierkes lend a hand.

Smoke and flames pour into the sky while observers sadly stand by and watch the conflagration.

With the fire extinguished, Batjac employees survey the damage. It was even rumored that the fire was deliberately set to destroy second-unit footage shot by John Ford. That was incorrect, however, as film canisters were never stored in that building.

The remains of the first floor, c. 2004.

On December 11, Wayne and Clothier filmed the exterior explosion of the chapel's south transept, the last major special effect shot of the film. A massive blast, this scene was a continuation of the powder magazine explosion sequence. Three Todd-AO cameras used to film the shot were structurally protected. One was manned by an operator; the others remote-controlled. A huge mortar charge was planted underground outside the south transept, and controlled fires were restarted in the magazine window and doorway. The special effects team chipped away plaster on the exterior walls, so explosive charges could be planted. Once rigged with wires to a central control panel, the detonation switches were thrown. As the scene began, debris started to fall out of a second hole, similar to the earlier triangular detonation seen in the magazine explosion. A third hole was created with additional debris seconds before the final explosion. Both holes were much smaller in size than the first. A frame-by-frame analysis of the effect indicates it isn't continuous; in that, the scene was spliced together—examination of the smoke formation, the color of the explosion over the fallen cross as well as the position and number of horsemen in the background all indicate a *jump cut*. A jump cut is a transition between two shots that seem to "jump" due to the

The massive secondary explosion of the chapel's powder magazine. A protected camera is visible in the middle of the photograph. Note that the explosion clearly occurs outside the building.

The three previously mentioned openings in the walls are visible. The demolished rear wall of the chapel can now be seen through the transept opening.

The now destroyed Alamo chapel. Scorch marks are seen on the façade.

way the shots are framed in relation to each other. The jump cut in the angle of the explosion was an attempt to bring the two explosions closer together, timing-wise, without cutting away. When the smoke cleared, two of the transept's exterior adobe walls had been knocked down and rubble creatively placed. (This was the opening through which Carlos Arruza and his lancers would enter the Alamo.) The left half of the apse's back wall was likewise razed. It's possible the transept wall was rigged to collapse simultaneously with the exterior explosion. Charges may have been planted over the entire side of the transept, and both the exterior mortar explosion and interior transept collapse occurred at the same time. In fact, a reddish-orange explosion can be seen *inside* the chapel seconds before the exterior transept blast.[96]

After *The Alamo* wrapped-up filming in December 1959, the set pretty much stayed in the same shape it was left in until the following year when production commenced on *Two Rode Together* although Happy's employees built a barrier out of railroad ties to keep cars from driving into the North Wall breach as well as the section of the West Wall that Wayne demolished. "Wayne spent all his money on the Alamo. And he blew the smithereens out of it," Shahan said. "I had to borrow a lot of money to build it back." Happy planned to rebuild portions of the Alamo that were blown away and even wanted to add a one-mile long "western" street to the village; hard to imagine that many buildings! Happy recalled, "I tried to get Wayne to go into business with me… when Wayne and I agreed on building the Alamo here, Wayne paid for the Alamo compound, period. He wanted to just build fronts. I told him not to destroy the village in the film, and I would give him a town, instead of fronts. I had in mind then what I wanted to do with the town after the film was completed. After this, I had a meeting with him and his two sons, Pat and Mike, in my house. I said to them, 'Here's what I want to do. I want to show you that we can make this a movie center. I want you to give me five thousand dollars, and we'll call this location John Wayne's Alamo Village.' We talked it over at great length, and John seemed very interested in the plan. When we were about through talking, Mike said, 'Daddy, why don't we just sleep on this tonight and talk to Happy tomorrow?' Well, I knew right then what Mike's attitude was, and the deal never came to be. I knew I could take Wayne's name and advertise it as *John Wayne's Alamo Village*. He'd own half of it, and I'd own half of it. I'd own the land, and we'd pay the ranch a dollar a year rental. But they turned me down. John said, 'Five thousand dollars; why should I put up anything?' I said, 'Why shouldn't you? I saw you lose eleven thousand dollars one night in just one throw of the dice in Vegas.'" Pat Wayne's recollection was slightly different. "I don't recall actually being at the meeting, although I know that a discussion took place. I remember that my father did not want to join the venture. He arrived at his decision independently. He did not need counsel from my brother. He was adamant about this. He wanted to destroy the set in the hopes that the village would never happen. To my knowledge, he never recanted on this decision." Although Duke, Michael Wayne and Happy had a long talk to discuss the proposal, they never could agree on the details and Wayne decided not to pursue it. (He felt Shahan could never attract enough tourists to make the offer profitable. "I can get people to come anywhere," Happy boasted. In later years, when he informed Duke that many visitors thought Duke owned Alamo Village, Wayne could only wryly reply, "I wish I did.") As a result of the aforementioned loan arrangement, Happy owned the village while Wayne owned the Alamo compound and church. However, once filming was over, Wayne found himself with a set he really couldn't do anything with. As Wayne stated, "We built the sets, then gave the whole thing away. They may make more money from it as a tourist attraction than we will from the picture." "If it's a flop," he joshed, "I'll have to change the billing to star, director, producer, bankrupt." Since Wayne rented the property from Shahan to build the set and then walked away from it, all the structures on the property reverted back to Shahan. More than likely, Happy probably picked up the remains of the Alamo compound set for free.[97]

The next series of photographs document the destruction of the Alamo set. The rubble-filled, fallen timber interior of the Alamo chapel. A breach in the rear wall can be seen through two timber poles.

As John Henry Daniels leads the mule, Aissa Wayne and Joan O'Brien pass the demolished Long Barrack.

The northeast corner of the Alamo compound, including the tree that burned in the film and the base of a corn crib at the right. This is after Happy covered the bare adobe walls with new plaster (darker portions). Reprinted with the permission of Richard Curilla/Alamo Village.

An exterior view of the northwest corner of the compound and North Wall breach.

Alfred Ybarra's jorno (oven)–a design trademark in his Westerns. The northwest cannon ramp is in the background.

The northwest cannon emplacement and the North Wall breach.

A portion of the destroyed West Wall.

A view of the Main Gate/South Wall and Alamo chapel. You can see damage to the "east" end of the Low Barrack, a partial view of Travis's headquarters, and the destruction to the "south" side of the chapel.

A better view of the South Wall. Travis's headquarters is seen in its entirety, as well as the demolished West Wall and the breach in the North Wall. Scorch marks are visible on the Long Barrack. Cannons, limbers and caissons surround the set.

An aerial view of the West Wall and remains of Travis's headquarters.

A view of the northwest corner of the compound and the North Wall breach. During the clean-up period after the film crew left, props were sold, temporary structures dismantled, and trailers and portable air-conditioners were removed and shipped back to Hollywood.

Although there has been some conjecture about just when Happy decided to open the Village to tourists, it appeared this idea may always have been in the back of his mind. "After (the) movie folks cleared the area, visitors clamored in for a look," Happy said. Visitors were welcomed and allowed to see the devastated remains of the set. In later years, he liked to say that the idea came to him when he was out mending fences for the third time because curious individuals kept cutting the wire to sneak in and see where the movie was filmed. As a result, Happy started to charge admission. The timing of this implies that the movie was already finished, so it had to be sometime after December 1959.[98]

He also had to hire caretakers for the Village as tourists were prone to taking "souvenirs" if not supervised. But in a late 1958 television interview with a *San Antonio Light* reporter and station KONO cameraman Bill Allert, Happy confirmed that after filming of the movie was completed, his intention was to "convert the movie set into a world-wide tourist attraction with shopping facilities and top-notch summertime entertainment." At that time, construction of the movie set was only about three-quarters complete. This was well over a year before the film actually wrapped. Asked what would become of the movie set, Happy said, "Well, we won't even start shooting until September of 1959, and I don't know when the picture will be finished. But when it is, all this will

"Welcome to Alamo Village. Home of John Wayne's "The Alamo," c. 2004.

be mine. All mine!" "But what will you do with it?" he was asked. "I don't know," Happy replied, "but I'll think of something." Initially, Happy had intended to use the second floor of the Hotel for dances. The cantina was to be used as a saloon, but only "red-eye soda pop" would be served. One of the three water tanks on the set would be turned over to fishermen. He was planning to bring in authentic Native American families to give demonstrations in weaving and in making silver jewelry and pottery. He also planned to halt motor vehicles within a certain distance of the buildings, and then bring tourists in the rest of the way by stagecoach. Saddles were going to be sold at the Slade Saddle shop while Julie's Original Bonnets would be available at the Trading Post. Western paintings by Bud Breen, one of the extras in the film, were going to be on display as well.[99]

Plans also were made to include the Aldridge Indian Museum. "All I wanted at first was a movie set, because I knew what I could do with it," Happy admitted. "I didn't conceive the idea of building a town until after we had built the fronts. Also, I had been collecting old junk and antiques for years, and I wanted a museum kind of place to put them in." At one time he had even contemplated having full-sized wax figures of Crockett, Travis and Bowie placed in the Alamo, along with the remainder of the defenders as well as the Mexican army.[100]

October 18, 1960. The trail ride to San Antonio for "The Alamo" world premiere begins on the Shahan ranch. The caravan included covered wagons, buckboards, carriages, and stagecoaches, with Indian and trail scouts in full costume. The trail ride ended on Monday, October 24 with a long parade in downtown San Antonio.

John Wayne spent an estimated $12 million on the production of *The Alamo*. He expected to get that back plus more when the movie was released. Happy Shahan, ever the businessman, planned on rebuilding portions of the Alamo that had been blown away, add a permanent soundstage, and expected Wayne's revenue to look like chicken feed when the set was finally turned over to the public.[101]

By the following year, Happy was well on the way to realizing his dream. In October 1960, while Wayne premiered *The Alamo* in San Antonio, John Ford was ensconced at Alamo Village filming *Two Rode Together* with Richard Widmark, James Stewart, Linda Cristal and Shirley Jones. For this film, the Alamo stood in for Fort Grant while the village was converted from 1836 San Antonio to the 1870s town of Tascosa, Texas. The Tascosa Hotel, a two-story building and soundstage, was added; in later years it would be known as the Wardlaw Hotel in honor of Lashawn Wardlaw, Happy and Virginia's granddaughter. Later, the village and Alamo would be modified and expanded for other movies that would be filmed there. A sheriff's office, jail and parson house were added for *Bandolero!* (1967), with the two-story makeshift soundstage Melroy building (named for Mel Tillis and Roy Clark) added for *Uphill All the Way* (1984). "This is the only self-contained cowboy movie place in Texas," promoted Shahan. "Within a 150-mile radius we got everything–prairie, bluffs, waterfalls, range land. We furnish the horses, buckboards, buggies, everything they want."[102]

When films weren't being made, Alamo Village was open every day for a 50¢ admission fee. (Fifteen years later, the price of admission increased to $3 for adults and $2 for children ages 6-12.) Mock gunfights took place in the streets; at times, trials were even held in the cantina with veteran western comic Curley Langston portraying the bartender-judge and a jury packed with tourists. Rudy Robbins handled the reins of a four-horse stagecoach that traversed the rolling hills of a cattle range, past prickly pear, Spanish dagger and prairie flowers, just as it was in the past. A two-day trail trip cost just $15 and you could camp out under the stars. The "largest cactus ranch in the world" with over one hundred fifty species was also created at the Village. Operated by Jack Thompson, botanists and horticulturists were invited to study the many varieties that could be purchased and shipped anywhere in the world. Happy even branched out into the newspaper business with the short-lived publication of the *Alamo Village Star*. So successful with these activities, he entered into a two-year contract with San Antonio-based public relations agency MasterCraft Incorporated, to "use its best endeavors to promote and maintain the success, reputation and interests of Happy Shahan." According to the wily Texan, one hundred thirty-one thousand tourists visited Alamo Village in 1961, with another one hundred twenty-one thousand the following year. Happy was on pace to entertain over one hundred fifty thousand in 1963 and within a few years, he predicted the annual number of visitors would reach two hundred fifty thousand! Sadly, it was not to be.[103]

But while it lasted, the Village's success enhanced the surrounding community. Visitors traveled from far and wide just to see the set that Wayne had built. Exclaimed Happy, "(When the movies come into town) it helps the cafés, dry goods stores, grocery stores, gas stations and even the common laborers getting jobs as extras." Along with spring and summer vacationers and tourists, the area received another annual economic lift each fall with the arrival of deer and turkey hunters. Said Vernor Bippert, Kinney County agent, "They start coming in ten days or two weeks before the season opens. For the ranchers alone, where these hunters hold leases, it means added income to their regular livestock profits." In addition to lease money, motels, hotels, restaurants and other businesses profited from the influx of hunters. And, of course, while there, everyone had to have a place to stay. Enter the Fort Clark Guest Ranch. Spread out over four thousand acres, the fort's services included a dining room, fifteen miles of trails for horseback riding, fishing, golf course, barbecue, skeet range and airport. And all for just $6 per guest at the motel barracks ($10 for two), or $200 if one wanted to stay in the spacious Wainwright House. With seven bedrooms, three baths, kitchen, dining room, living room, servant's quarters and serving pantry, it could accommodate up to fourteen guests. Shahan's trait of slight exaggeration must have been contagious–local advertising bragged that the Driskill Hotel company had converted the enlisted men's barracks into "plush 'motel-type' rooms and the officer's quarters into equally modern guest cottages. A maximum of 375 people can be accommodated in the 180 rooms, which range from a large, comfortable room with private bath and twin beds for two people on the European plan to the gigantic Wainwright house."[104]

Happy's humanitarian streak was in evidence as, later that year, Alamo Village hosted a Hollywood auction, barbeque and rodeo, the proceeds going to purchase a desperately needed ambulance for Kinney County. While local businessmen donated items ranging from goats to power mowers, movie stars including Wayne, Rock Hudson, Jayne Mansfield, Sandra Dee, Jennifer Jones, Robert Taylor, Jill St. John, Bobby Darin, Kim Novak, Jack Lemmon and Linda Cristal provided personal items for sale such as books, wardrobe and jewelry. It was a rousing success.[105]

So were the annual Labor Day events: horse races with both male and female contestants, Pony Express relay races with a mail bag serving as a baton, Western gunfights, Indian dances, trick-horse shows, and a barbeque dinner served on paper plates. The horse races covered 250, 300, 400 and 800 yards while The Pony Express race was 1½ miles. A championship race was run in a 440-yard dash; the winner received an Alamo Village silver loving cup. The following is a typical broadside…

"The Annual Cowboy Labor Day horse races mark the highlight of the season each year at Alamo Village. Any cowboy riding saddle who feels his horse can win is invited to enter. Excluded are stud horses, race horses that have been on the track, and registered horses. Races will get under way immediately following the Texas-style Outdoor Barbecue lunch. Aside from the races, Alamo Village offers rides aboard an authentic stagecoach, horseback rides, a shooting gallery, and plenty of time for browsing through the museum-type walk-ins and picture gallery. Live entertainment is planned for the entire day. The funny, witty and talented Roni Stoneman, banjo pickin' star of Hee-Haw fame (1977), along with Texas' own Dotsy (Brodt), RCA recording artist with current chartbuster "After Sweet Memories Play Born to Lose Again," will team up and are set to entertain the guests at the 17th Annual Labor Day Cowboy Horse Races at Brackettville. Joining Dotsy and Roni Stoneman will be Edna's Richard Vasquez, the Texas Twisters, and a cast of Alamo Village Stars. Seguin's Clark Grein and the Eezy Riders Band, who were a tremendous hit at last year's Alamo Village Labor Day festivities, have been summoned to return for this year's events. Other guests include Jim Brewer, Nashville VIPS Bob and Charlene Bray, and Cecil Davenport, Entertainment Coordinator for the christening of the USS TEXAS nuclear cruiser. Bring the family and plan to spend the whole day…"

Sadly, 1962's events turned tragic when Bill Moody's horse, Charlie Faust, failed to rein in after winning a thrilling three hundred fifty-yard race and plowed headlong into a stagecoach tongue and harness. Bill slammed his head and shoulders against the body of the coach and fell beneath its wheels. Acting instinctively, Rudy Robbins raced to prevent the horses from stampeding and dragging the coach over the unconscious rider. Moody suffered a concussion and numerous fractures; though Charlie fell, he only incurred a cut on his eye.[106]

In later years, Shahan entered the promotion business. As he had cut a few records in his younger days, country music seemed a logical choice so he established Celebrity Management, Inc. in Nashville. Two of his successful protégées were Dotsy Brodt and Johnny Rodriguez. Explained Happy, "By having the ranch, we got the movies. By having the movies, we got the tourists. So when I started the tourist business, I decided I had to have entertainment. But why should I hire entertainment to come out here and just leave? I decided to hire entertainers that have possibilities, and then I train them and put them out on the market. I saw the bright lights when I was young. I get my thrill now from helping people. I'm tough on 'em, but I'm for 'em, and they know that. And that's how I get my kicks."[107]

Now if you're interested, the Village is up for sale. As Happy used to say, "Of course it's for sale. Just make me an offer. But I don't really care whether I sell it or not." In 1963, Happy was approached by Maxon, a Midland, Texas, real estate company, with an intriguing question: how much would it take if someone wanted to buy his home, Alamo Village and ten thousand acres of his ranch? The answer: $2 million. The realtors said they thought they could get it. Although he refused to identify them, Maxon's Jack Bentley said, "We have two nationally known persons interested." But, the deal fell through. Interestingly, it was offered as an ultimate gift in the 1971 Sakowitz Christmas catalogue. For the princely sum of just $3 million dollars, a well-heeled Christmas shopper could purchase the Alamo movie set and all its contents. The Houston specialty department store had previously advertised such items as A.J. Foyt's winning Indianapolis 500 race car as well as a pollution-free home in a giant environmentally controlled air bubble. For the person who wanted to get away from life in the big city, the movie set was the perfect gift. Said Robert T. Sakowitz, executive vice-president of the store, "Everybody talks about getting away and where they can go. Everybody wants a country place or a ranch. Now, someone can have a town. It is not only for the man who wants to own the town, but for the man who wants to make decisions on the spot. He should have no law and order problems since he's the sheriff. It is a gift for a man of action and for an ambitious man who wants to prove there is some rugged individuals left in the country." The purchase price included one square mile of ranch land (640 acres) and, according to Sakowitz, "the living quarters were ready for the new owner: 'It is paneled, has inside plumbing and air-conditioning… very plush. We'll even equip it with some bourbon and branch water.'" For those who have ever visited these "plush" quarters, suffice to say Sakowitz slightly exaggerated.[108]

This particular Christmas "gift" was never purchased, so in April 1973, Happy listed the movie set and nine thousand acres with the Johnson and Inks Real Estate firm from Llano, Texas. Although all reasonable offers would be considered, once again, the village remained unsold. In January 1975, Saudi Sheik Al-Aharis Al-Hamdan attempted to buy the real Alamo. It seems his son had visited San Antonio and was taken with the beauty of the building and, since he loved his son, he wanted to purchase it as a present. Texas governor Dolph Briscoe immediately said, "No dice," but Shahan wasn't deterred. Happy rushed off to the telegraph office and wired, "Take my Alamo." Virginia was more blunt: "It's for sale any time he wants to haul it over there." There was no reply. No matter. St. Louis brick dealer Bud Boldt had his own plan. Upon a paint factory being demolished, he'd acquired a full-sized terra-cotta reproduction of the Alamo façade. "I didn't know what it was at the time," confessed Boldt. "But I wanted it for the beautiful terra cotta work. I told my friend that if I could have the façade, I'd take his lousy bricks." Asked about the price, Boldt said, "Well, he is a sheik. I guess he could afford just about anything." Apparently the sheik wasn't amused.[109]

When he wasn't trying to sell the Alamo, Shahan tried to sell his collection of antiques. In 1977, Happy hosted one of his many Western Auctions. Held over the weekend of September 17/18, hundreds of items from his collection were offered. Advertised as "some of the best and oldest antiques known in the Western world," items ranged from wagons to saddles, stagecoaches to pianos. A saloon bar, glassware, furniture and cash registers. Longhorns, spurs and arrowheads. For those movie buffs, the auction also included such items from Wayne's film as wagon wheels, adobe bricks and a bed Aissa Wayne used in the film. The latter was purchased and now is displayed at the Whitehead Memorial Museum in Del Rio.[110]

Over the years, fewer and fewer major productions were filmed at Alamo Village. After *Bandolero!* in 1967, Happy waited another thirteen years before *Seguin* with Edward James Olmos and *Barbarosa* with Willie Nelson came along in 1980. During the interim there were occasional documentaries, Western shorts, informational films and television variety shows filmed there, but, by that time, Happy was tired and ready to sell the village once again. This time, he increased his price to $4 million, which included a section of land, the Alamo set and village and everything contained within. "Anybody in the world can buy Alamo Village who has the money," said Shahan. Regardless, whether he sold the town or not, Happy said that 1980 would be the last summer the village would be open to tourists. He wanted to discontinue operations to devote more time to raising longhorns and such other pursuits as managing several musical performers. He also planned to stage two or three longhorn sales a year plus perhaps an art show featuring bronze statues. In 1980, one group had an option to lease it by November 1 after the doors closed September 30. But, "if they don't lease it, then there'll either be someone (to) buy it or we'll continue operating it like a private commissary," said Shahan. "We're changing its image. We just want to make it a town that helps us in our other businesses. It (the tourist business) takes five months that I'm just doing the public a favor. I'm not making any money. Our intention is to make it much more flamboyant, more lucrative and more worldwide known. Tourists can also come when we're making movies." He was already in negotiations with a production company to film another Alamo movie on location: *Thirteen Days of Glory*.[111]

But once again, he didn't sell or close up shop. In fact, more major movies with more major actors were filmed there in the '80s than ever before: *Up Hill All the Way* (1984) with Roy Clark, Mel Tillis and Burt Reynolds; *Houston: The Legend of Texas* (1986) with Sam Elliott and Katherine Ross; *The Alamo: 13 Days to Glory* (1986) with James Arness, Brian Keith, Alec Baldwin and Raul Julia; *Alamo the Price of Freedom* (1987) with Casey Biggs; *Lonesome Dove* (1988) with Robert Duvall and Tommy Lee Jones and *Gunsmoke: The Last Apache* (1989) with James Arness, Michael Learned and Richard Kiley. According to former public relations director Lashawn Wardlaw Melvor, the set was open even when filming was under way. The only star who wouldn't film there because of that policy was Elvis! And the 1990s were just as successful: *Rio Diablo* (1992) with Kenny Rogers, Travis Tritt and Naomi Judd; *Bad Girls* (1993) with Madeline Stowe, Andie MacDowell, Drew Barrymore and Mary Stuart Masterson; *The Gambler: Playing for Keeps* (1994) with Kenny Rogers and Mariska Hargitay; *James A. Michener's Texas* (1994) with Patrick Duffy and Stacy Keach; *The Good Old Boys* (1994) with Tommy Lee Jones, Matt Damon and Sam Shepard; *Streets of Laredo* (1995) with James Garner and Sissy Spacek; *Once Upon a Time in China and America* (1996) with Jet Li and *Bullfighter* (1999) with Willem Dafoe and Olivier Martinez. And yes, Alamo Village was still for sale. As Happy said, "It's been for sale since the day it started. Make me an offer."[112]

By the mid-90s, Happy's poor health at last caught up with him. A frail gait and stiff right arm eventually slowed down the life-long entrepreneur, no longer allowing him to ride his beloved horses: "My neck and arm are in bad shape. I can't do any lovin' or fightin'," he said humorously.[113]

Sadly, on Tuesday, January 30, 1996, Happy passed away and Virginia then took over operation of the village. "Virginia was the backbone for her husband's never ending pursuit to promote Bracketville and their world famous movie set. (She) picked up the torch and continued (Happy's) work in promoting not only local tourism but tourism all over Texas." Noted author and historian Frank Thompson recalled that a few months before Happy passed away, Frank was asked to discuss the possibility of helping Happy write his autobiography. "I knew he had been approached by several people to do so," recalled Frank, "so the fact that he wanted me was a great compliment. We sat down in the office behind the gift shop to talk things over and he began regaling me with stories of his life. Periodically, Virginia (who was busy with gift shop business) would come through the room. She'd listen for a moment to whatever Happy was saying, shake her head and say, 'That's a lie!' and then leave." A great story and a great woman.[114]

On the weekend of May 23-24, 1998, Virginia held a once-in-a-lifetime *Alamo* reunion on the anniversary of John Wayne's birthday. "(We have) long wanted to have a reunion, but for one reason or another it just never happened," she said. "Then, when Duke's Hollywood Cowboys called and asked if they could come to the village and celebrate (Wayne's 91st birthday), we decided the time was right for a reunion. We have tried to plan the event so people of all ages will enjoy it." In addition to the Cowboys, a group of professional and non-professional entertainers, fans, and celebrity look-alikes, the event featured Dean Smith, Rudy Robbins, Joan O'Brien, Bill Daniel, Bill Moody IV and Pilar Wayne. Emma Hernandez, Rosita Fernandez (flamenco dancers), and Ricci Ware (Tennessean) also were there. That Saturday evening kicked off with a good old-fashioned Fandango with music provided by the Alamo Village Bunkhouse Band, Dave Crowe, Ermal Williamson as John Wayne, and Rudy Robbins and his Spirit of Texas band. Teresa and Willie Champion (El Curro), who also appeared in the film, entertained guests as well. Texas singer/songwriter John Rutherford, a personal friend of Pilar's, also was present. Tommy Worrell, stuntman and quick-draw artist, performed with his pet longhorn, Sundance, and the Spirit of Texas band along with Los Flamingos dance troupe entertained throughout the day. Pilar, an accomplished artist in her own right, signed lithographs of her own paintings and autographed her biography. At noon, a free Texas-style BBQ was served, followed by an auction of film memorabilia. The highlight of that Sunday's activities was a star-studded panel discussion. It was the first time all the film's celebrities had gotten back together since filming ended in 1959.[115]

Virginia continued to hold the annual Fourth of July and Labor Day festivities, historical re-enactments, trail rides, weddings, field trips, gunfighter competitions, Western Fandangos, hayride and cattle drives. Only the names and faces changed. Each year friendships were rekindled, memories revisited, stories enhanced. But those associated with the film grew fewer and fewer. Typical of the re-enactments was the one held in 1976 on the one hundred fortieth anniversary of the battle; sponsored by the National Re-Enactment Society, the Texas Army and Alamo Village, the Mexican Army of General Antonio Lopez de Santa Anna (including NRS soldiers of the Dallas Light Artillery, the Austin Re-enactment Society, Austin's Co. E, Fourth Texas Infantry, the Lancers de Jalisco from New Orleans, Beaumont's Eighth Texas Cavalry, and the Fourth Tennessee Cavalry) once again stormed the walls of the Alamo (defended by the Texas Army and the NRS Gonzales Volunteers). Almost two thousand five hundred press representatives, television cameramen, tourists and visitors were on hand for the event.[116]

But events associated with the film eventually grew fewer and fewer. In 2001, Virginia again listed the village for sale. She asked $6.5 million for the 500-acre set and said she had "several bites." Asked about previous inquiries to buy the set, Virginia confessed, "A lot of people asked, but I always ignored them. It's the movies. I won't believe it until somebody walks through the gates with the money." By 2004, however, the negotiations were "kind of in limbo. I hope they keep it like it is. We're still active, and we want to stay active." In October 2005–the forty-fifth anniversary of the premiere of *The Alamo*–the film again was shown (Alamo Village had hosted a previous outdoor showing on April 3, 2004) in the one spot it was meant to be shown–outside, under the stars, within the adobe walls of the Alamo set. Fans from all over the world were there, as were members of the Wayne family: Marisa Wayne (Duke's youngest daughter) and Anita and Don LaCava (his granddaughter and son-in-law). The rousing complement of supporting members included Dean Smith, Rudy Robbins, Jim Brewer, Marshall Jones, Robert Harris, Teresa and Willie Champion, Bill Hart and Tommy Worrell. The film, complete with overture, was shown on a huge inflatable screen. Storm clouds gathered during the evening, no doubt, held off by Duke until the film was over.[117]

But time waits for no one, and on June 23, 2009, at ninety-three years of age, Virginia passed away. Seven days later on June 30, after years of entertainment and filmmaking, Alamo Village closed its doors. The following statement notified a shocked public:

"With the passing of Texas Icon, Virginia F. Webb Shahan, a difficult business decision has been made by family members. Alamo Village is closed to the general public. Our gates have been open to the visiting public and to the film industry for fifty years. At this time, we choose to close the gates of Alamo Village in order to reconstruct management and possibly redirect our efforts toward new positive goals. The future possibilities for this historical movie set are many. At present time, managers and owners continue with sound decision making even in the midst of a troubled economy. Our future goal includes the pursuit of continued business relations within the film industry, producing more and even larger trail drives and promoting individual group tours. As decisions are finalized, announcements will be made to the general public.

"To the multitudes of visitors, businesses, employees and dear friends who have contributed to the success of Alamo Village throughout these five decades, we offer our heartfelt gratitude and a sincere Texas thank you. God Bless us one and all."[118]

The ranch was bequeathed in equal shares to the three Shahan children: Tully, Tulisha and Jamie. Upon completion of a feasibility study, Alamo Village was opened again to the public. Sadly, Tulisha passed away just three months later on September 26 and the village was once again closed. However, "…in response to constant requests from travelers and buffs wishing to photograph the sets, walk the famous streets, and stand on the ramparts of John Wayne's Alamo," in March 2010 it reopened briefly for six months–for three days a week, with limited hours and no shows, stores or food services–all for a $10 admission fee. According to Rich Curilla, "We were just letting people come in and walk around." But even this was to no avail because finally on August 28, 2010, Alamo Village, Inc. issued this statement: "After a valiant attempt to keep Alamo Village available to visitors on a limited basis, the family has made the painful decision to close it permanently. This will be effective immediately. Family and management alike wish to thank all those who have contributed their hearts, talents and hard work to Alamo Village over the past fifty years." Jamie Shahan once placed the movie set on the market but has subsequently removed it. As of this writing, the movie set remains closed to the public although still occasionally available to carefully selected productions. It is by no means "an abandoned western movie set" as has occasionally been cited in the press. There is the possibility, however, that an enterprising individual may still purchase the site and, once again, transform this shabby, rock-strewn village into the magnificent setting it once was. Perhaps there's a rancher from Dallas, an oil baron from Houston, or maybe even a retired owner of a construction company from Corpus Christi, who has a vision. A vision of a good old-fashioned Western town with saloons, jail and a hotel. A Western hotel you could spend the night in. Or, for the less adventurous, a more modern one complete with running water. Barns and stables where you could rent a horse, or board your own if you're so inclined. A narrow-gauge railroad complete with wood-burning locomotive. Christmas decorations in the winter, flags and bunting on the Fourth of July. Horse and foot races. Stagecoach rides and a shooting gallery. Good, wholesome family entertainment for one and all. Maybe even a barbershop quartet. And a full-sized soundstage to attract the film industry. A town created and built on Western values, American values. A town folks would be pleased to raise their children in. Who knows? God willing and the creek don't rise, one day it just might be possible.[119]

Alamo historian Dr. Bruce Winders expressed everyone's feelings when he said, "Alamo Village had been a popular stop for Alamo fans for years. To many, it was more 'real' than the actual site. For people in the Alamo community, the closing of the village is like the passing of a friend."[120]

Today, the set is slowly crumbling down around itself as Mother Nature and time continue taking their toll. Cracks have widened in the church facade, trees overgrown in the courtyard, walls and structures mere shadows of their former selves. Weathered signs and broken adobe litter the set. But for those who had the opportunity to visit it in its heyday, Alamo Village will always remain fresh in our memories–a shining beacon to three good people–Happy, Virginia and Duke: never forgotten, always in our hearts.

Alamo Village is located seven miles north of Brackettville on FM 674. Take U.S. 90 west from San Antonio and drive 124 miles or so thru Castroville, Hondo, Sabinal and Ulvalde before you reach Brackettville. Turn right at the light on FM 674. Fort Clark Guest Ranch is on the left hand side of U.S. 90, 150 yards before you reach this light.

The following is a photographic history of Alamo Village. It is not the author's intent to detail each and every building, year by year or film by film. Rather, this overview will give readers a fair understanding of how Alamo Village has changed over the last five decades. Where necessary, explanations will be provided for various photographs but it is assumed by now that if you've reached this point in the narrative, you probably already have a fair working knowledge of the Alamo set. Many of these photographs have been provided by members of the johnwayne-thealamo.com forum. For those interested in John Wayne and/or the cultural/historic and/or cinematic Alamo, this is THE forum to visit. Gratitude and appreciation are given to the following individuals for providing these photographs: Tony Pasqua, Ned Huthmacher, Kevin Young, Richard Curilla, Kristi Hale, Craig Covner and Alamo Village.

San Fernando Church, Front Street, c. 1961.

Front Street, c. 1961 after "Two Rode Together." The church has freshly painted trim. AV

The railing on the hotel was removed in 1968 after "Bandolero!" The balcony roof you see now was added in the 70s. The stagecoach may have been from "Two Rode Together." NH.

Back Street, mid-'60s. Happy hasn't added his office in the back of the Cantina yet. AV.

The Cantina, early '60s. No liquor, just pop! AV.

Front Street, c. 1962. The Alamo Village Trading Post is now established in the Hotel. A new Cantina sign was painted to replace the one removed by John Ford for "Two Rode Together." AV.

A rear view of the church, c. 1962. The adobe wall and archway in the front of the building were removed for "Bandolero!" The Mexican gazebo between the church and Hotel Tascosa was built for "The Alamo." AV.

The Tascosa Hotel, "Two Rode Together." NH.

The front of the Stage Depot, c. 1962. AV.

Cemetery, c. 1966. NH.

Happy rests in front of Gilman's Livery stable, c. 1967. AV.

The Cantina with the "Bandolero!" facelift; the First Bank of Val Verde is on the right. AV.

The "Bandolero!" Plaza in 1968. The sheriff's office on the far left has been re-plastered; Happy is on the horse. AV.

A wonderful view of the Tascosa Hotel, c. 1976, which is currently used for wagon storage. AV.

This photograph was taken on Back Street through the passageway between the Cantina and Bank, c. 1968. Initially constructed in 1960 as the Tascosa Hotel, it was given a facelift for "Bandolero!." AV.

The Trading Post, Cantina and Val Verde Bank, c. 1980. The square, plastered adobe pillars were added in 1967 and built around Ybarra's cedar posts. CC.

Front Street after the "Bandolero!" facelift. AV.

Front Street, post-1988. KY.

San Fernando church, c. 1975. KY.

Cantina and Trading Post, c. 1975. The Cantina still had Ybarra's porch roof on it, which was replaced in the early '90s. KY.

An aerial view of Front Street, taken from an official Alamo Village postcard, c. 1986.

Parson's House. Built as a background for the hanging sequence in "Bandolero!," Happy converted this "false front" set into a four-sided structure with concrete foundations, c. 1993.

"Saddles" for sale, c. 1993.

The Stagecoach Barn, c. 1993.

The backroom of the Cantina where John Wayne delivers his "Republic" speech to Laurence Harvey, c. 2007. The door on the far left leads into Happy's office.

The Cantina fireplace into which a drunken Tennessean is thrown, c. 2007.

184 | *Alamo Village: How a Texas Cattleman Brought Hollywood to the Old West*

Back Street, c. 1975. KY.

A view of the Wardlaw Hotel on Front Street, c. 1975. The extension of the Cantina to accommodate Happy's office is on the right.

A view down Back Street from behind the scalloped cemetery wall, c. 2010.

Ruined Back Street arches, c. 2010.

An added-on porch to the back of the Trading Post, c. 1986. The fluted wooden columns and their heavy wood capitals were saved from the "Bandolero!" Cantina set. The flower pots on the window curb are set dressing items left over from "The Alamo." NH .

Virginia's Hotel (the rear of the Alamo Village Trading Post), c. 2010.

For those who remember the scene in "The Alamo" where a rather large peasant woman climbs into a doorway, this is the building, c. 2012. The original signage read "Frijol – Arroz – Garbanzo."

An interior view of the Low Barrack, c. 1961. It has already been whitewashed and the profile of the jagged parapet over the Main Gate has been squared-off for "Two Rode Together."

The Alamo chapel and remains of the Long Barrack, c, 1961. NH.

The Long Barrack, c. 1962. The "fallen" cross stills stands behind the chapel parapet. In 1967, the palisade was removed for "Bandolero!" and replaced with an eight-foot-high adobe wall to mask Alamo Village, which represented the village of Val Verde. The palisade subsequently came and went, built again in 1986 for "Houston: The Legend of Texas," removed and rebuilt a month later for "The Alamo: 13 Days to Glory," and again removed and rebuilt the next year for "Alamo: The Price of Freedom." NH.

The following several photographs show what the Alamo compound looked like after "Bandolero!" was filmed there in October/November 1967. The compound's open plaza was transformed into the village of Sabinas, while the well in the photograph would later be defended by Alec Baldwin in "Alamo: 13 Days to Glory." Wayne's flagpole mound was leveled and its caliche strained and recycled into adobe bricks used to build the Alamo Village jail. The cantina on the right is a three-sided set, the remainder contained part of a fourth wall in the back and a removable wild wall. NH.

The buildings on the left were just false adobe fronts on concrete foundations. They faced the Long Barrack and were built by Chato Hernandez down the middle of the Alamo compound, starting with the cantina set just inside the main gate. NH.]

The lower level of the Long Barrack, artistically chipped to give it an aged appearance, is on the left side of this photograph. NH.

The infamous "$7,500" wall that Happy built. Seventy-five hundred dollars because that is what Happy would tell film companies it would cost if they wanted to remove it. While you can still see the façade and the hole in the powder magazine wall, the remainder of the chapel is in ruins. A three-element arcade, made of wood and plastic, was unsuccessfully used to camouflage the front of the chapel. In an additional effort, the Alamo's all-too-familiar parapet was knocked down to alter its appearance, but Happy insisted it be replaced after filming. NH.]

An interior view of the Alamo chapel, c. early '70s. The sagging cannon platform is supported by a splintered telephone pole. For those brave enough to try, a ladder seen on the left was available. TP.

"Bandolero!" ruins, c. early '70s. Except for the well in the plaza, all "Bandolero!" sets were removed in 1980 for "Barbarosa." NH.

Partial remains of the West Wall as seen from the north end Long Barrack steps, c. 1973. The northwest cannon ramp can be seen at the far right. NH.

An interior view of the Alamo chapel, c. 1973. While the cannon platform and ladder are still intact, only one roof arch remains. This arch survived into the '80s but by 1987 the interior of the chapel, or what remained of it, was rebuilt for "Alamo: The Price of Freedom."

Several of the following descriptions are from sketches made by Ned Huthmacher at the time. By 1974, the south wall of the baptistery had collapsed, exposing the inner chamber and weakening the cannon platform. The Low Barrack roof was no longer safe and its staircase was closed to the public. NH.

A view of the demolished West Wall; Travis's headquarters still hasn't been repaired, c. 1974. The West Wall was rebuilt to a certain degree for "Barbarosa" in 1980, albeit with false fronts. NH.

The east wall of the baptistery has now partially collapsed and a crack developed on the Alamo chapel façade, running from an upper window to the arched door, c. 1975. NH.

The Alamo chapel in profile, c. 1975. NH.

The Alamo compound Convento courtyard gates. The crumbling remains of the chapel can be seen in the background. NH.

Looking from inside the baptistry (powder magazine) of the Alamo chapel across the nave to the confessional room, c. 1975. The chapel doors are to your left. Behind you is a large hole in the wall, a result of the magazine explosion. NH.

The North Wall, c. 1975. From left to right: remains of the West Wall, the northwest cannon ramp, a wooden cannon platform in the center of the North Wall, the burning tree. KY.

The next six photographs were taken in 1976. The Alamo chapel; remains of the "Bandolero!" set are visible on the far right.

Remains of the West Wall. CC.

A view of the back of the Alamo set. Trees, shrubs and vegetation have begun to take over. CC.

The remains of the monk's burial room on the north side of the Alamo chapel. Bowie's room lies through the doorway and to the left. Richard Widmark's death scene was filmed near the buttress. CC.

Gate to the Long Barrack courtyard. CC.

The rear stairs of the Long Barrack as viewed from the Convento courtyard. Upstairs floor joints are all that are left of Travis's headquarters. CC.

In 1977, the Alamo chapel's cannon platform collapsed and was removed. By 1980, the east wall of the sacristy and a portion of the chapel's south wall had also collapsed. Once again, the Low Barrack roof and staircase was closed to the public. The back of the Alamo chapel, March 1986. A false back wall was added to make the chapel look intact for filming. NH.

The next six photographs show how the set looked for "Houston: The Legend of Texas," (aka "Gone To Texas") and "The Alamo: 13 Days to Glory." Both of these movies were filmed in 1986. In fact, just as the "GTT" production company was leaving, the "13 Days" crew was arriving. Refurbishing of the compound was a joint effort by both companies. The Main Gate, c. 1986. Those are Ybarra's original doors from "The Alamo." Over the years, they have been removed for "Barbarosa" and "Rio Diablo" (1992) but always re-hung. LG.

A view of the Alamo chapel and Long Barrack after filming was completed. The fake structure to the left of the chapel was built for "Barbarosa" in 1980. A tile patio was also laid down from the sacristy opening all alongside the Long Barrack. Though most of it was removed for "13 Days to Glory," some still remains.

The Long Barrack as seen from the southwest cannon platform. NH.

The Alamo chapel. The palisade was removed in anticipation of the arrival of "13 Days." NH.

A view of the main gate. NH.

The "13 Days to Glory" palisade before it was removed for "Alamo: The Price of Freedom." NH.

The next six photographs represent the condition of the movie set after "Alamo: The Price of Freedom" was filmed in 1987. The Alamo chapel's profile has been modified to represent a more historically correct appearance. NH.

An interior view of the Alamo chapel. Note the stuffed-cowhide barricade. NH.

The North Wall, complete with vertical timber revetment. NH.

The main gate lunette. Although not historically correct in configuration, "POF" was the first Alamo film to include this defensive feature. NH.

The Long Barrack.

Travis's headquarters along the West Wall.

The Alamo compound, c. 2001. Travis's headquarters was transformed in 1992 into what is now semi-affectionately known as "The Pink Hump" for the film "Rio Diablo." NH.

The following six photos were taken by Kristi Hale and represent the current condition of the Alamo set. The chapel facade.

Arches in front of the "Pink Hump" and the northeast corner of the compound.

The Main Gate stairway.

An anteroom next to the Main Gate. The exterior wall has deteriorated to such a degree that daylight can now been seen through the adobe.

The burning tree in full foliage.

Trees and shrubbery are slowing taking over the compound.

Sadly, these last four photographs focus on the ruins of the West Wall and northwest cannon emplacement. What were once sturdy adobe structures are now just wooden shells, slowly crumbling, to be lost forever.

210 | *Alamo Village: How a Texas Cattleman Brought Hollywood to the Old West*

Appendix A: Selected Alamo Village Buildings Constructed in 1959

Much of the following information has been derived from Alamo Village story boards, written by Richard Curilla, Al Ybarra's original village 1958 blueprint, and physical verification.

noun ado·be \ə-ˈdō-bē\: A type of brick made of a mixture of mud and straw that is dried by the sun. Adobe construction is usually referred to as non-engineered construction because engineers and architects are not involved. Generally, it's a simple rectangular construction with a single door, and small lateral windows. If there is a foundation, it has to be relatively strong to bear the weight of the adobe blocks. Walls are made with blocks joined with mud mortar and usually never rise above two stories. Sometimes, blocks in the corner are laid over each other in a crossing pattern to assure structural integrity. A lintel is placed above door and window openings to support the blocks above it. The roof can be made of wood joists resting directly on the walls or supported inside indentations on top of the walls. Roofs are generally *azoteo* (terraced) in style–a slightly pitched roof within the walls that raised parapets two or more feet above the surface of the one- to two-foot thick roof, or could also be covered with a gabled wooden framework of cedar posts with *tule* (river weeds) bundled into *fascines*. These were often built over failing *azotea* roofs. *Canales* with long exterior spouts (two to four feet) drained water out one side of the roof and spouted it beyond a narrow flagstone sidewalk (in the towns). Ybarra, of course, built mostly *azotea* roofs. Roof covering can also be corrugated metal sheets, wood or clay tiles. Mud, lime plaster, whitewash or stucco is applied to interior and exterior walls.

Everything built as set faces for the camera was made of adobe brick on poured concrete footers. All sides of all buildings on the Cantina side of Front Street are completely adobe as are the restrooms at the far end of Back Street, the Veramendi Palace (soundproofed to house an electrical generator), the small house next to it with the partial palisado front (it had only a partial back), and the corner building on the other side of the back gate. The only parts of the set that have wooden backs are the buildings (all one building) between Wayne's office and the restrooms, and the west face of the end building on Front Street. They were designed only as background, and the west and north walls of them are all wood.

"Bowie's" Room (28): A one-story, dirt floor, 28´ x 32´ adobe-walled building (including an 8´ x 20´ roofed porch), with single-gabled, weathered shingle roof. This structure was built and used for Richard Widmark's opening scene with Jester Hairston. The building has windows on both the front and side walls, a blocked door on the back wall across from the front door, and a small, shuttered, pane-less window in the upper portion of a forty-five degree beveled corner. Green lattice covered a jagged breach in the back wall. The back door and windows offered access for the crew behind the camera as well as ingress for all necessary cables and wires. The film's *interior* shots were filmed in this building, but all *exterior* shots were of the back of building 16 across the street.

Cantina (9): The 30´ x 60´ single-story, wooden-frame structure remains much the same as it was after construction in 1958 although the bar, stage and kitchen were added after filming ended. The copper-topped, brass-railed bar, originally from San Francisco, found its way to Texas after the former's 1906 earthquake, where Happy acquired it in the early 1960s from a saloon in Fredericksburg. The faux staircase was added in 1984 for the film *Uphill All The Way*. The wooden stage, now in its third iteration, initially stood where the kitchen door is next to the fireplace; the second version went from corner to corner in the alcove and had a diagonal apron that faced the main entrance. The kitchen was also created in the early '60s from two areas: a passageway that went from a door under the front roof porch through to Back Street, and the aforementioned first stage. The door to the passageway was not present when the building was initially constructed but may have been added as the script evolved. Ybarra's front porch was replaced in the early '90s with the current shingled roof supported by telephone poles. Happy's back office, which is not accessible to tourists, was constructed in the early- to mid-'60s. Sadly, green signage painted throughout the exterior of the building can no longer be seen as it was either painted over or simply faded away.

The Cantina interior. Reprinted with the permission of Kristi Hale, c. 2012.

For those interested in such things, it appears that the "morning-after" scene with Flaca and Crockett was initially planned for a porch in the rear of the Cantina. Explains Alamo Village historian Richard Curilla, "…the angle of the Bexarenos leaving that we see in the movie immediately after the scenes of Santa Anna's army approaching 'over mountain and plain' was designed to be Crockett's POV (point of view) from the balcony of his room. His window was across the balcony from Flaca's window, as originally planned. This window relationship still exists over the back door of (the) current Cantina kitchen and is clearly dramatized in the screenplay. My conclusion is that the scene, where he sees Flaca stretching and then goes to her window, was originally staged for this set and later actually filmed on the front veranda. In addition, the structure of the set built in connection with Flaca's bedroom interior in the airplane hangar at Fort Clark was meant to duplicate this rear window and the roof/balcony above (the) kitchen door and NOT the window on the front veranda. That's why it faces the length of the balcony in the movie rather than straight out from the front of the building."

And, for those REALLY interested, the rear of the Cantina seen in the film was NOT the original design. Initially, all that was there was a very short-lived, pitched, wooden porch roof, supported by four cedar posts, which ran the length of the back of the building. It's possible that the aforementioned script change also necessitated this change as well. Ybarra then must have eliminated the posts, enclosed the area with walls and included a green, lattice-covered arched window. This newly-created room now enclosed an adobe partition wall, fireplace and the adobe wall of the alcove where the current stage is.

Cast Building aka John Wayne's Batjac office (26): A single-story, two-room, 23′ x 50′ adobe building with poured concrete floor and pitched red tile gabled roof–one of only three such buildings in the village (the San Fernando church and an un-named house across from the church that was covered with straw thatching for the film are the other two. In later years this building housed the Johnny Rodriguez Museum and County Jail.) Located on Back Street and identified as *Comanderia de Policia* (police station), the building, one of the few on the set that was air-conditioned, served as Wayne's command center and included a front office for Mary St. John, a rear office with lavatory for Wayne, and a separate lounge area for cast members. In a poor attempt to camouflage the window-mounted air-conditioning unit, Ybarra painted it green. Although the building only appears for four seconds in the film, the A/C unit stands out like a sore green thumb.

Hotel San Antonio (11): Like most of the village's structures, this building served multiple purposes. Though it obviously represented a lodging establishment in the film, when not used as such, its first floor was filled with row upon row of costumes, while the second floor served as a dining hall for cast and crew. At 33′6′′ x 70′8′′, the wooden structure wasn't terribly spacious but large enough for nine 20′ dining tables, three to a row. A roof was added to the porch in 1969/70. The Hotel was a two-story building with multiple window/door openings on both levels. The upper level consisted of six openings: unshuttered windows on both the far left and far right sides of the building, with four shuttered openings in between. The first shuttered opening on the left was a doorway, the remaining three openings were windows. A second-story wooden balcony extended across the face of the Hotel, enclosing the doorway and three center windows, with three-foot-high (est.) front and side banisters/railings. The balcony was constructed of wood with floor boards running parallel to the face of the building. A forty-five degree exterior staircase ran from lower-right section of the first floor to the upper-left section of the second floor. The staircase opening on the second floor was also protected by a wooden banister/railing. The overall width of the balcony appeared to be about ten to twelve feet. Other than the open doorway on the left side of the balcony, there was no other hallway, alcove or wall extending out from the right side of the balcony, wild or otherwise. None of the windows appear to have a barred grate except the one that Crockett looks into when Emil Sand and Flaca argue. The first floor had four openings: two grated windows, a doorway and another window. The square plastered adobe pillars were added in 1967 and built around Ybarra's cedar post supports. The interior of the building was not used to film any scene, either on the first floor or second floor. All interior scenes in the building–whether in the hallway, inside Flaca's room, or outside looking into the room–were filmed at an off-site sound stage located in a Fort Clark airplane hanger. And yes, the extremely large oleander bush in front of the Hotel is the same one that was there back in 1959!

San Fernando Church (15): Designed by Al Ybarra, this multi-roomed adobe structure consisted of three units: a 40′ x 23′ nave, a 22′ x 24′ antechamber used for the "basement" scenes, and a 22′ x 13′ bell tower. A wooden floor was placed on top of the antechamber with a ledge that extended out beyond the walls with a belfry and cupola constructed on top of that. In an early draft of the script, gunpowder was to be stored in the bell tower. Upon discovery by Crockett et. al., the upper portion of the church would be destroyed in a massive explosion. One could assume that the entire upper structure would have been removed and rebuilt out of Styrofoam adobe for this explosion scene. However, once Wayne and Shahan sorted out Duke's financial situation and ownership of the village subsequently reverted back to Happy, the scene was re-written so that the gunpowder was instead removed from the basement of the church. An archway and adobe wall that used to jut out into the plaza from the front of the church was removed when *Bandolero!* was filmed in 1967. If you're fortunate enough to have the back doors of the antechamber opened, you'll see exactly how the basement scene was filmed, complete with stairs leading down from the bell tower.

For those wanting to know exactly just what *does* remain of the original 1959 Alamo compound, sadly, there isn't much. Over the years, numerous Alamo and non-Alamo-related movies have been filmed here, each slightly, or in some cases not so slightly, modifying Wayne's set. *Houston: The Legend of Texas*; *The Alamo: 13 Days to Glory*; *Alamo–The Price of Freedom*; *Bandolero!*; *Bad Girls*; *Two Rode Together* and many others have all taken full advantage of this unique set. But for those with a sharp eye, Ybarra's magnificent original work can still be seen:

- The main gate/Low Barracks, although squared off and modified for *Two Rode Together*, including original gate and stairs, *southwest* corner and cannon ramp.

- The chapel's front façade and adobe *north* wall is still the original although it's now pierced with a doorway to the outside, and the *east* wall of the current inside room is the original wall that Widmark died just beyond.

- The arched wall from the church to the Long Barracks.

- The convent courtyard walls behind the Long Barracks (including the gates) and stairs leading to the back of Travis's headquarters.

- Part of the lower portion of Travis's headquarters although it is covered with a wooden set and arched front entrance. The second-story south wall is original to waist-high and covered with plaster.

- The *north* portion of the Long Barrack, including the two-story end building complete with wooden stairs.

- The bathrooms are original, although initially only a front baffle wall. Wayne added doors, windows, back and side walls when he realized he needed facilities for the extras.

- The L-shaped building of the *northeast* corner of the compound as well as the timber *North wall* rifle platform.

- A short portion of the wall that extends from the platform toward the *northwest* corner of the compound.

- The two cannon ramps leading to the center and *northwest* corner of the wall.

- The now crumbling interior center portion of the West Wall. The wall only remains in the form of façade of the eastern side. Except for slight mounds of earth under the POF West Wall, all walls and partitions are gone.

Appendix B: Composition and Construction Method of Fort Clark/Bracketville Buildings in 1959

(The following information is derived from the National Register of Historic Places, Nomination form for Fort Clark.)

Designed as a typical military complex, structures were arranged around a parade ground used for maneuvers measuring approximately 1680´ x 700´ with the long axis oriented NE/SW. The parade ground was bisected with a road into two fields, one for foot maneuvers and a larger one for mounted maneuvers. Commissioned and non-commissioned officers' quarters were located along the west side of the parade ground while commanding officers' quarters were located on the south side. Barracks for enlisted men were constructed along the east and north sides and administrative structures were placed in the area east of the parade grounds. The original fort headquarters building (ca. 1870) and a fort movie theater (ca. 1918) were added. Medical facilities were constructed in the south corner facing the parade ground (ca. 1880). Although construction of the fort spanned a period of approximately sixty years, the structures compromising the main body of the complex are integrally related to one another and the parade ground, and appear as components of a whole rather than individuals. While designs vary, characteristics common to all contribute significantly to the cohesion of the group. Solidly massed in simple geometric configuration, the one- and two-story buildings are constructed of native limestone obtained from fort property. They are sturdily built for function and endurance with a minimum of applied decoration.

The earliest structures were built using a palisade type of construction in which cedar picket posts set in double rows and infilled with rock and plaster form walls. The Palisado (ca. 1855) is the only remaining example of this method and is believed to be the oldest existing structure at the fort. By the late 1850's buildings were constructed primarily of load-bearing masonry. Variations of cut stone and construction methods are evident in buildings whose dates span from approximately 1857-1940.

The headquarters building (ca. 1857) displays walls of dressed limestone blocks, finely chiseled with sharply defined edges. Textured with subtle tool marks, the blocks are bonded with thin, regular mortar joints. Exaggerated sills define the doors and window openings and a large rectangular block with simple bolection bracket and construction date carved in relief accentuates the entrance.

Solid stone construction with less refinement was employed in many of the buildings erected during the 1860s and 1870s including the enlisted men and officers' quarters. The blocks have a more irregular shape, rougher surface, and less clearly defined edge than those used on the old Headquarters building. In addition, the doors and windows feature wooden rather than stone lintels. Constructed along the west and south sides of the parade ground, the officers' quarters (ca. 1870) consist of two-story structures made to accommodate two families each with identical floor plans on either side of a dividing wall. Large porches with diagonal bracing… enhance the front facades and dormer windows pierce the steep-pitch gable roofs. The interiors were finished with milled lumber brought in from San Antonio and Bastrop. Located across the parade ground, the enlisted mens' barracks (ca. 1870) consist of single-story rectangular structures with low-pitched gable roof extend to form a porch across the front façade. A single-story, rectangular detached kitchen and mess hall with the long axis perpendicular to the barracks was constructed behind each barracks although only four remain (ca. 1870).

A third type of masonry construction is exhibited in the Commissary Building (ca. 1880). The two-and-one-half story rectangular structure is fabricated in rusticated ashlar offset with a string course of pitch-faced ashlar between the first and second floors. *(Ashlar is finely dressed (cut, worked) masonry, either an individual stone that has been worked until squared or the masonry built of such stone. It is the finest stone masonry unit, generally cuboid or less frequently trapezoidal.)* The doors are defined by segmental keystone arches and the windows feature exaggerated sills and lintels, all of smooth cut, tooled limestone. Located northeast of the parade ground, the commissary is the most visually arresting of the fort structures. The main (south) façade features a central bay which rises above the hipped roof to form a third floor. Intersecting the roof on all sides are dormer windows topped with pitched roofs and enclosed with fish scale shingling. A two-and-one-half story projecting portico composed of unadorned vertical posts with diagonal bracing and criss-crossed balustrade spans the full width of the south façade. Simple wooden stairways incorporated into the portico provide access between floors.

Twentieth century construction on the fort continued to acknowledge the abundance of locally available stone although the method of construction varied from that of the earlier buildings. Erected in 1915 in the northwest corner of the parade configuration, the Noncommissioned officer's club is built with a frame structure veneered with an irregular cut field stone and a tooled mortar joint. The U-shaped barracks along the north end of the parade ground (ca. 1930) are also of frame construction with field stone veneer. The Officers' Club Open Mess, currently known as Dickman Hall (named after career cavalry officer Maj. Gen. Joseph T. Dickman (1857-1927)), served Fort Clark from 1939 to 1944 and later became the Guest Ranch Headquarters. The site of the future Officers' Club was built upon the ruins of the Post Trader's store. In 1939 this site of the first post commissary and quartermaster storehouse, on the prominent ridge which overlooks Las Moras Creek and the bridge which leads onto the fort, was chosen as the location for the new Officers' Club. During the 1950s and 60s the Brown Foundation, through the Driskill Hotel in Austin, operated the grounds as the *Fort Clark Guest Ranch* and used the building as Ranch Headquarters, dining room and lounge.

Northwest of the parade area the lush bottomland where Las Moras Springs emerges from below ground has been developed for recreational purposes. The springs collect in a large shallow pond bordered with concrete. Water flows through a large, natural bottom swimming pool surrounded with foliage and also through a concrete channel besides the pool into Las Moras Creek (ca. 1940). Retaining walls and flower boxes were built of fieldstone and the area around the

Fort Clark Historic District, Brackettville, Kinney County, Texas. Reprinted with the permission of Friends of Fort Clark Historic District.

pool was landscaped and equipped for picnic and play. In the area are three single-story structures: restrooms, a bath house, and storage facilities. Though modern in design and materials, the small units are inconspicuously sited between the large trees of the creek area and are far enough removed from the main body of the fort that they do not jeopardize its architectural integrity. A pump house constructed beside the spring pond is today enclosed by a cyclone fence. The two-story white stucco building with contrasting posts and lintels bears little resemblance to the structures surrounding the parade ground (ca. 1919) however, substantially removed from the concentration of stone structures, the stuccoed building does not intrude on the architectural continuity."

(The following alphabetical descriptions of selected buildings/areas are taken verbatim from various Kinney County Historical Commission Monographs and historical markers.)

Las Moras Spring: As the ninth largest spring in Texas and the largest spring in Kinney County, Las Moras Spring is significant due to its location and invaluable natural resources. *Moras*, meaning "mulberries" in one Spanish translation, refer to the mulberry trees found along Las Moras bank. The spring discharges an average of 12-14 million gallons per day. Archaeological objects such as flint points and burned-rock middens demonstrated that prehistoric people frequented Las Moras. In historic periods, the area was occupied by Coahuilitecan Indians, hunter-gatherer tribes in the Lower Pecos region, Apache, and Comanche. These groups stopped at Las Moras Spring while on trails into Mexico. The annals of New Spain 1590-1771 record Europeans such as Gaspar Castano de Sosa, Fernando del Bosque, General Alonzo de Leon and Field Marshal Señor Marqués de Rubí traveling to the spring. On October 13, 1840, Republic of Texas troops under Major John T. Howard attacked and destroyed a large Comanche village here at the spring. In 1848, Texas patriot Sam Maverick claimed the spring as part of his headright survey. By the next year, travelers on the new military road from San Antonio to El Paso were using the spring as a regular resting place for wagons bound for California. Fort Clark was established on June 20, 1852. The U.S. Army walled the spring pond in 1902 and created a swimming pool fed by the spring. The present pool was constructed for the Army in 1939 through the Works Progress Administration (WPA) and is the largest ever built on any post. Las Moras Spring, supporting over eleven thousand years of human life, demonstrates the role of ecology in Texas' development.

Fort Clark swimming pool, c. 1920s.

Fort Clark: A strategic installation in the U.S. Army's line of forts along the military road stretching from San Antonio to El Paso, Fort Clark was established in June 1852. Located near natural springs and Las Moras Creek, its site was considered a point of primary importance to the defense of frontier settlements and control of the U.S.-Mexico border. Many infantry regiments and almost all cavalry regiments were at one time based at Fort Clark, as well as companies of Texas Rangers and Confederate troops during the Civil War. The Army's Seminole-Negro Indian Scouts also were assigned to Fort Clark, and with Black troops of the Tenth Cavalry and Twenty-fourth and Twenty-fifth Infantry played a decisive role in the Indian campaigns of the 1870s. Prominent military leaders who served here include Col. Ranald S. Mackenzie, Gen. Wesley Merritt, Gen. William R. Shafter, Gen. John L. Bullis, Gen. Zenas R. Bliss, Gen. Jonathan M. Wainwright, and Gen. George S. Patton, Jr. Fort Clark remained a horse-cavalry post for the U.S. Army through World War II and finally was inactivated in 1946. The fort property, including many native stone buildings constructed by civilian craftsmen in the 1870s, was listed in the National Register of Historic Places in 1979.

Front gate to Fort Clark, c. 1930s. Reprinted with the permission of William Haenn/ Warren Studio, Del Rio, Texas.

Adjutant's Quarters: Erected during the 1873-1875 expansion of Fort Clark to accommodate and support an entire regiment, this structure differs from other quarters on the line in that it is a single dwelling rather than a duplex. The Fifth Regiment of the U.S. Cavalry was garrisoned here from 1921 to 1941 and during that time the Regimental Adjutant, who performed essential clerical duties for the Regimental Commander, lived within these walls. The core of this building is a three-room hall and parlor plan composed of adobe, featuring a symmetrical front and stone chimney at each end. Additions were made in 1904 and 1944.

Commanding Officer's Quarters–Wainwright House: Fort Clark was established as a U.S. Army garrison in June 1852. Nine structures designed by U.S. Army engineers were built in 1873-1874 to house the fort's officers. This house served the fort's commanding officers, including Col. Ranald S. Mackenzie and Gen. Jonathan M. Wainwright. Architectural features include a central entry, wood-frame porch, six-over-six windows, second floor dormers, and four large chimneys with sculpted caps. Recorded Texas Historic Landmark–1963.

Guardhouse: Established in 1852, Fort Clark was manned by varying troop strengths over the years. This guardhouse was built in the 1870s during a period of fort expansion. A new stockade was built in 1942 to relieve overcrowding, and the guardhouse became headquarters for the military police. Built of limestone blocks, the building reflects an adoption of military design to local materials and climate, and retains its 1930s appearance.

Post Guardhouse, c. 1896. Reprinted with the permission of William Haenn/ Robert J. Sporleder, Fort Clark Historical Society.

Infantry Barracks–1873: By 1873, Fort Clark had grown to regimental size, compelling construction of six single-story infantry barracks and three two-story cavalry barracks by the U.S. Army Quartermaster Department. This one-story rectangular plan barracks was built of coursed rubble limestone with a gable wood shingle roof, stone fireplaces, central roof vent and shed front porch. The open interior housed bunks for sixty-four soldiers with a single gun rack in the center of the open bay. The company barracks faced the officers' quarters to the west across the parade field. Today this building is the best surviving example of its kind at Fort Clark, and one of a handful of Indian Wars period barracks left on any post in the nation.

Married Officer's Quarters: This single-story duplex once served as housing for married officers and their families at Fort Clark. The U.S. Army fort, established in 1852 to defend the western frontier of Texas and the border with Mexico, saw significant growth in the 1870s. To accommodate a regimental size garrison, the Army constructed living quarters such as this particular house. Built by 1875 out of uncoursed, rough-cut limestone, the building features a cross-hipped roof, interior chimneys with double fireplaces and a distinctive U-shape. The fort closed in 1944 and later owners transformed the quarters into a single family home.

New Cavalry Barracks (1932): This structure served as quarters for the enlisted men and women of the fort's garrison. A state-of-the-art facility complete with self-contained mess hall, finished basement with offices, supply rooms and latrines; three 30´ x 65´ open bays for bunks and wall lockers with hardwood floor and beaded board ceilings. The building was constructed of hollow tile, veneered stone finish, concrete flooring and asphalt shingle roofs. Built on the site of the 19th century Quartermaster Storehouse, the building would later house the 1855th Women's Army Corp (WAC) Service Unit in WWII. (Includes Patton, Bullis and Seminole Hall).[121]

New Cavalry Barracks, c. 1932. Reprinted with the permission of William Haenn/ Warren Studio, Del Rio, Texas.

Patton Barracks, c. 2014.

Officer's Club Open Mess–Dickman Hall: This building served Fort Clark from 1939 to 1944 and was named "Dickman Hall" after career cavalry officer, Maj. Gen. Joseph T. Dickman (1857-1927). It was reserved exclusively for officers and provided a place where they could take their meals and socialize. The building was constructed by Taini Construction of Del Rio, Texas with Phillip Garoni acting as site supervisor. As evidenced by the original floor plans the ground floor archways were all open forming the porch entrance. A lounge, dining room, tap room, kitchen, guest room, maid's room, and four rooms for visiting officers' quarters occupied the first floor. The second floor featured an airy ballroom with a hardwood dance floor, the only such amenity for miles around. The two-story building has a main hipped roof with gabled roof bays flanking a central arched portico entrance. A web-walled stone veneer clad frame and clay tile construction. During the 1950's and 60's the Brown Foundation, through the Driskell Hotel in Austin, operated the grounds as the Fort Clark Guest Ranch and used the building as the Ranch headquarters, dining room and lounge.[122]

Officer's Quarters 2, 3 and 4: These buildings date from 1854-55, soon after the U.S. Army established Fort Clark. The antebellum fort then included officers' quarters and barracks for enlisted men, as well as a two-story quartermaster storehouse, powder magazine, hospital, guardhouse and post headquarters around a parade ground. During this period, such notable army officers as John Bell Hood, J.E.B. Stuart, Fitzhugh Lee and James Longstreet served here and likely lived in these quarters. Horizontal logs and vertical posts were notched and interlocked to create these buildings. Limestone chimneys are also historic. The army closed the fort in 1944, by which time the buildings were clad in lath and plaster and wood siding.

Officers' Row Quarters: Fort Clark was established as a U.S. Army garrison in 1852. The original quarters were crude log huts and houses of palisade construction. In 1857, a new program began to replace badly dilapidated structures with buildings of quarried stone. Designed and constructed in 1873-74 as duplexes to accommodate two officers' families each, these eight residences closely resemble those built on other military posts during that time period. The buildings reflect an evolutionary adaptation of military design suited to local construction materials and the regional climate. Each duplex has three large rooms on each floor, two fireplaces and a fifty-five-foot front porch. An 1885 remodeling project changed the houses from rectangular to T-plan. The Army contracted with Central Power and Light Company for electricity in 1918. Fort Clark was deactivated in 1946 and sold to the Brown and Root Corporation. In 1971, the fort property became "Fort Clark Springs", a private recreational community. The officers' houses were rented to members and guests until 1974, when they were offered for sale to members of the Fort Clark Springs Association.

Quarters No. 16-17, c. 1895. Reprinted with the permission of William Haenn/William Hilderbrand, Gainesville, Texas, from glass negative.

"Colony Row. C. 1960s."

Palisado: Erroneously identified as the Robert. E. Lee Courthouse, this 1869 structure was originally a kitchen and mess-room for the stockade. Later it served as a company storeroom, tailor shop, and amusement hall. The two-room, hipped-roof building is diagonally braced at the corners and features a stone fireplace at one end. Its interior walls are lined with tin employing flatten fuel cans. This structure was built by the U.S. Army in 1869-70 and is an example of vertical post or jacal construction, used due to the absence of trees tall enough for traditional horizontal log construction.[123]

Post Cemetery: This ground was Fort Clark's military cemetery from 1856 to the 1880s. One of the first burials was 2nd Lt. Brayton C. Ives, First Infantry, a West Point graduate who died here on June 27, 1857. Succeeding burials included dozens of military personnel, dependents, and civilians. Pvt Peter Corrigan, Fourth U. S. Cav., the only casualty of Col. Ranald S. Mackenzie's raid to Remolino, Mexico, was laid to rest here in May 1873. In 1880, a second cemetery opened south of the main post and this site became inactive. All burials here were reinterred at Fort Sam Houston National Cemetery in 1946. A historic limestone wall encloses the space. Some original headstones have been preserved.

Post Theater (1932): This structure replaced an earlier building that served as a church, theater, courtroom and recreation center. A utilitarian military design of clear span construction, brick wall and stucco veneer, the building also exhibits classical style influences in its pilasters, arched windows, and pediment. A popular movie theater until the fort was closed in 1944, it later became a town hall for the Fort Clark Springs community.[124]

Post Theater.

Regimental Headquarters: A one-story, U-shaped, wooden structure built in the 1930s by Taini Construction. It was removed from the post in 1947.

Service Club: The building served as a morale and welfare facility; a place of rest and relaxation until 1944 when the U.S. Army closed the fort. From 1949 to 1980 the building was used as the Brackettville Country Club. The Service Club occupied the site of the first post guardhouse and was constructed in 1938 by Taini Construction. The one-story structure has a rectangular plan with gabled roofs. The foundation is limestone web-wall with a wooden frame superstructure sheathed with horizontal siding. Windows are typically wood four by four casement. A stone porch adjoins the front entrance at the east façade. The south wall has a wood frame extension with a hipped roof which returns to the south wall of the body of the building. Between the higher gabled roof and extension roof are a series of stepped wood louvered vents.[125]

Signal Corps Building: This building served as the communications center for Fort Clark from 1932-1944. The building is of tile brick construction with a veneer of irregular cut field stone. The original footprint was enlarged (ca. 1940) to accommodate barracks for enlisted soldiers. During World War II mobilization, the Third Signal Troop of the Second Cavalry Division and the signal detachment of the 1855th Service Company shared this building and maintained the post telephone system, army training film library, post photo lab, and other essential equipment. The Signal Corps detachment were the last troops to leave Fort Clark when it closed on August 28, 1944.

Staff Officers' Quarters: The U.S. Army built nine stone officers' quarters at Fort Clark beginning in 1873. The need soon arose for additional housing for senior staff officers, and this building was constructed in 1888. Built in a T-plan, the two-story stone duplex features a full width front porch and is a good example of military standard housing adapted to the materials and climate of the region. Among the house's residents was General George S. Patton.

BRACKETTVILLE:

Brackettville School House: a four-room, weatherboard, one-story frame structure, with green shutters and roof. A white picket fence with four stiles, one in the middle of each side, enclosed the grounds.

Carver School Grounds: When Fort Clark's Seminole-Negro Indian Scout Detachment was disbanded by the U.S. Army on September 30, 1914, the Seminoles were required to relocate to Brackettville. They held school in their church until new grounds were purchased by the Brackett Independent School District in March 1919 from J.F. Maddux for the purpose of providing a site for a "colored school" for Brackettville's Seminole-Negro community. The old Maddux homestead, a two-story limestone structure built in 1870, served as the building for the school, which was named George Washington Carver School. The first floor was used for classrooms while the second floor was leased to the Black Masonic Lodge until 1923. In 1930, the structure was condemned as unfit and unsafe for school purposes. The second story of the building was thus removed in 1944 and first floor was remodeled inside and stuccoed on the outside. The building was again used as classrooms for the primary and elementary grades while high school classes were conducted in a new building completed in early 1944 by the 162nd Engineer Squadron of the Second Cavalry Division then stationed at Fort Clark. At the time, Carver School was the only accredited Black school between San Antonio and El Paso. The Seminole Indian Scout Cemetery Association was deeded the school grounds by the Bracket I.S.D. in November 1965. The original stone schoolhouse has since served as a meeting hall and cultural center for the Brackettville Seminole Community, including local Juneteenth celebrations and Seminole Day each September. The 1944 building now serves as classrooms for the community Headstart Program.

Dolores Townsite: The only settlement founded in John Charles Beales' ill-fated Rio Grande colony of 1834-1836. Beales (1804-1878)–empresario of 70 million acres in present Southern and Western Texas and New Mexico–was Texas' largest known land king. In 1833 he and a partner brought fifty-nine settlers here to colonize a town to be named for Beales' Mexican wife. Indian raids and drought soon took their toll, but the death blow came in 1836. As the group fled the Mexican Army during the Texas Revolution, Comanches killed all but seven of one party. This ended the town's existence.

Filippone Building (1885): Italian stonemasons Giovanni B. Filippone (1845-1917) and Giovanni Cassinelli purchased property here in 1883-85 and in 1885 built the six-sided portion of this limestone block building. Filippone became sole owner in 1887 and operated a general store on the first floor, while his family lived on the second floor. The five-sided, one-story section was added early in the 20th century. Abandoned by the 1940s, the Filippone building underwent rehabilitation in the 1990s and now stands as an important reminder of Brackettville's commercial heritage.

Kinney County Courthouse (1911): Human inhabitation of Kinney County began thousands of years ago. Spanish expeditions through the area began in 1535 and continued throughout subsequent centuries. An attempt at establishing a Franciscan mission in 1775 failed, as did settlement by Dr. John Charles Beales in 1834. Despite the hardships found in the area, Kinney County was carved out of Bexar County in 1850, two years before the U.S. Army opened Fort Clark as a frontier outpost. That same year, in 1852, local inhabitants established the Brackett settlement, named for Oscar B. Brackett who set up a stage stop, freight office and dry goods store to service the stage line from San Antonio to El Paso. Named for early settler and adventurer Henry Lawrence Kinney, Kinney County did not formally organize for twenty-one years; officials first met in Brackett's home in 1873. Brackettville, as the town had come to be called, was chosen as the county seat. Subsequent meetings were held in the Kartes and Co. building until 1879, when the county's first courthouse was built. The county used the 1879 building, which later housed a post office and Masonic lodge, until 1911. That year, the county first occupied this courthouse, designed by L.L. Thurmon and Co. of Dallas. Falls City Construction Co. of Louisville, Kentucky, served as General Contractor. Constructed in the Beaux Arts classical style, this domed cupola structure was built with octagonal corner towers and columned entryways. Its banding and corner quoins are accented with D'Hannis red brick.[126]

Kinney County Jail: Kinney County's first jail, a small square simple stone structure built by James Cornell in 1873 and torn down in 1922, stood across Ann Street on the courthouse grounds, where the flagpole now stands. This second county jail was accepted by the commissioner's court on January 20, 1885 and was at the time the finest stone building ever constructed in Kinney County. The Gothic revival style building was designed by the architectural firm of Wahrenberger and Beckmann of San Antonio and built in 1884 of ashlared limestone blocks by John Waite at a cost of

Kinney County Courthouse.

Kinney County Jail, c. 1885. Reprinted with the permission of William Haenn/ Zack Davis.

$16,000. The jail was remodeled in 1936-37 including removal of the second story due to structural damage from a series of disastrous storms. This durable building served as the county jail for ninety-one years, until 1976, when it was replaced by the law enforcement complex on North Street. Subsequent uses of the building include a dental clinic and the county nutrition center.

Las Moras Masonic Lodge Building: Built in 1878-1879 to serve as the first county-owned courthouse for Kinney County, this structure served that purpose for thirty-two years. In 1911 it became the headquarters of the Las Moras Masonic Lodge, which was chartered in 1876. While the Lodge used the second floor, the ground floor was leased to the U.S. Postal Service for the Brackettville Post Office from 1918 until 1983. Over the years, the building has also served as office space for Kinney County government departments.

Montalvo Building (1887): Yldefonso Montalvo (1855-1941), also known by the name Obed Woods, built this dwelling about 1887. He used cedar pickets, caliche plaster, and other materials available in the area. Originally the kitchen and several outbuildings stood nearby. The educated son of an English mother and Mexican father, Montalvo was a rancher and an employee of Fort Clark and a local mercantile store. He and his wife Guadalupe (Reschman) (1868-1953) and their nine children lived here. Built of cedar pickets, caliche plaster and other local materials, this two-room structure housed nine children. A community well in the back yard provided water for townspeople.[127]

Partrick Hotel (1885): In 1885 Dr. William Partrick commissioned adjoining commercial spaces at this site. The east side single story functioned as a notion and drug store, while the west side was a grocery and dry goods store. The second floor served as a hotel. Later outbuildings included a beer vault, windmill, elevated tank and bake oven. Dr. Partrick sold the property to R. Stratton & Co. in 1913. The Partrick building exhibits the skill of local stonemasons in rough-cut ashlar limestone blocks and finished limestone lintels and windowsills. By the 1950s, a suspended wooden awning replaced the original metal balcony and a stabilizing concrete veneer at the base addressed recurring flood damage. This building was constructed on a post and beam foundation entirely of rough-cut limestone blocks except for the front elevation which incorporates ashlar limestone of exceptional quality. Today, the ground floor, once *W.R. Partrick Drug Store & Fancy Notions*, now serves as the *Brackettville Funeral Home* operated by Humphrey Funeral Directors of Del Rio. The second-floor hotel is a two-bedroom apartment.[128]

All footnotes that reference Rich Curilla result from oral conversations with or written communications from Rich Curilla at Alamo Village. Without his cooperation and encouragement, this book would not have been possible. Physical verification of actual scene placement was conducted in September 2003, April/September 2004, May/July 2005 and October 2015.

The book that you are reading is the result of many years of research. Unfortunately, many of the principal characters in the production of this movie are no longer with us and, as memories fade over the years, it was extremely difficult to reconcile different stories, impressions and information. As a result, all errors of fact, omission and misinterpretation, if any, are the sole responsibility of the author. All comments should be directed to jkfarkis@earthlink.net.

Bibliography

Manuscript collection:

    BH   Brian Huberman, Rice University, Houston, Texas
    FTC Frank Thompson and Craig Covner
    TTU Texas Tech University, Southwest Special Collections Library
    USC University of Southern California

Interviews, Oral Histories and Personal Correspondence:
All interviews without an institutional affiliation were conducted by the author.

    B.J. Burns
    Don Clark
    Tim Cumiskey
    Richard Curilla
    Elaine Davis
    Henry Fuentes
    Ralph Gonzales
    William Haenn
    Chris Hale
    Chuck Hall
    Robert Harris
    Jose Hernandez III
    Mary Hernandez
    Brian Huberman
    Alan Kreiger, Jr.
    Bill Moody IV
    Ken Pruitt
    Jamie Shahan Rains
    Robert Relyea
    Rudy Robbins
    Chuck Schoenfeld

James Tullis "Happy" Shahan, BH, FTC, TTU
Tully Shahan
Virginia Shahan
Plunker Sheedy
Margarita Talmantez
Crystal Harvey Wade
Tulisha Shahan Wardlaw
Al Ybarra, BH, FTC
Joe York, Jr.

Books:

Clark, Donald and Christopher Andersen. *John Wayne's The Alamo. The Making of John Wayne's 1960 Epic Film.* Hillsdale, Illinois: Midwest Publishing, 1994.

Davis, Ronald L. *Duke: The Life and Image of John Wayne.* Norman, Oklahoma: University of Oklahoma Press, 1987.

Eyman, Scott. *John Wayne: The Life and Legend.* New York, New York: Simon & Schuster, 2014.

Fagen, Herb. *Duke–We're Glad We Knew You: John Wayne's Friends and Colleagues Remember His Remarkable Life.* New York, New York: Citadel Press, 1998.

Farkis, John. *Not Thinkin'…Just Rememberin'…The Making of John Wayne's The Alamo.* Albany, Georgia: Bear Manor Media, 2015.

Haenn, William F. *Fort Clark and Brackettville: Land of Heroes.* Chicago, Illinois: Arcadia Publishing, 2002.

Hansen, Todd. *The Alamo Reader–A Study in History.* Mechanicsburg, Pennsylvania: Stackpole Books, 2003.

Huffines, Alan C. *Blood of Noble Men: The Alamo Siege and Battle: an Illustrated Chronology.* Illustrated by Gary Zaboly. Austin, Texas: Eakins Press, 1999.

Lemon, Mark. *The Illustrated Alamo: A Photographic Journey.* Abilene, Texas: State House Press, McMurry University, 2008.

Munn, Michael. *John Wayne–The Man Behind the Myth.* New York, New York: New American Library, 2005.

Pritle, Caleb III and Michael F. Cusack. *Fort Clark: The Lonely Sentinel On Texas's Western Frontier.* Austin, Texas: Eakin Press, 1985.

Relyea, Robert. *Not So Quiet On The Set: My Life in Movies During Hollywood's Macho Era.* New York, New York: iUniverse, Inc., 2008.

Roberson, Chuck with Bodie Thoene. *The Fall Guy: 30 Years as the Duke's Double.* North Vancouver, British Columbia, Canada: Hancock House, 1980.

Roberts, Randy and James S. Olson. *John Wayne–American.* New York, New York: Free Press, 1995.

Rothel, David. *An Ambush of Ghosts: A Personal Guide to Favorite Western Film Locations.* Madison, North Carolina: Empire Publishing, 1990.

Schoelwer, Susan Prendergast. *Alamo Images–Changing Perceptions of a Texas Experience.* Dallas, Texas: Degloyer Library and Southern Methodist University, 1985.

Shepherd, Donald and Robert Slatzer with Dave Grayson. *Duke: The Life and Times of John Wayne.* Garden City, New Jersey: Doubleday, 1985.

Thompson, Frank. *Texas Hollywood-Filmmaking in San Antonio since 1910.* Perryton, Texas: Maverick Books, 2010.

Uecker, Herbert G. *The Archaeology of the Alamo.* Bulverde, Texas: Monte Comal Publications, 2001.

Wayne, Aissa with Steve Delsohn. *John Wayne My Father.* New York, New York: Random House, 1991.

Wayne, Pilar with Alex Thorliefson. *John Wayne: My Life with the Duke.* New York, New York: McGraw-Hill, 1987.

List of Newspapers:

Alamo Journal, The
American Cinematographer
American Heritage
Austin American, The (Austin, TX)
Austin American Statesman, The (Austin, TX)
Big Spring Daily Herald, The (Big Spring, TX)
Brackett News, The (Brackettville, TX)
Brackett News Mail, The (Brackettville, TX)
Chicago Tribune (Chicago, Il)
Columbus Daily Telegram (Columbus, OH)
Cuero Record, The (Cuero, TX)
Daily Texan, The (Austin, TX)
Dallas News, The (Dallas, TX)
Dallas Morning News (Dallas, TX)
Del Rio News-Herald (Del Rio, TX)
Fact, The (Brazos, TX)
Fort Clark, The Texas Post Return (Brackettville, TX)
Fort Worth Star-Telegram (Fort Worth, TX)
Galveston News, The (Galveston, TX)
Hill Country Herald (Leakey, TX)
Hollywood Reporter, The (Hollywood, CA)
Houston Chronicle, The (Houston, TX)
Houston Post (Houston, TX)
Llano News (Llano, TX)
New York Times (New York, NY)
Paris News, The (Paris, TX)
Pasadena Independent (Pasadena, CA)
San Angelo Standard Times (San Angelo, TX)
San Antonio Express (San Antonio, TX)
San Antonio Express-News (San Antonio, TX)
San Antonio Express and News (San Antonio, TX)

San Antonio Light (San Antonio, TX)
San Antonio Standard Times (San Antonio, TX)
Southwest Times (Fort Smith, AK)
Texas Co-op Power
Texas Highways
Texas Monthly
Times-Picayune, The (New Orleans, LA)
This is West Texas
Victoria Advocate (Victoria, TX)

Newspaper articles and Periodicals:

Allen, Nelson. "Remembering 'The Alamo.'" *San Antonio Express-News*, September 16, 1989.

Ashford, Gerald. "San Antonio Celebrates 'The Alamo.'" *San Antonio Express and News*, October 23, 1960.

Bacon, Joyce. "S.A. Cast at Brackettville. 'Alamo' Film Set Visited." *San Antonio Light*, July 16, 1959.

Banks, Jimmy. "Ancient Fort Now Guest Ranch." *Dallas Morning News*, October 8, 1961.

Beutel, Paul. "Remember the Alamo!" *Austin American Statesman*, May 29, 1977.

Blakely, Mike. "Alamo Village - The stuff westerns are made of." *Texas Highways*, May 1985.

Blumenthal, Ralph. "The Alamo of the Big Screen Tries to Skirt the Fate of the Original." *New York Times*, March 26, 2004.

Byrd, Sigman. "The Texas Rancher Who Will Inherit a Make-Believe City." *The Houston Chronicle*, October 15, 1958.

Campbell, Scott. "Footsteps, voices of stars echo through Alamo Village." *Unknown newspaper*, June 4, 1980.

Carlile, Tom. "'Alamo' Memories." *New York Times*, October 4, 1959.

Cary, Renwicke. "Around the Plaza." *San Antonio Light*, September 4, 1959.

Castillo, Ed. "About Town." *San Antonio Express and News*, August 23, 1959.

Chemerka, William. "Rudy Robbins." *The Alamo Journal*, June 2007.

Clapp, Marjorie. "Bexar Comes to Life." *San Antonio Light*, mid-to-late, 1958.

Crowe, Dave. "The Shahans." *Hill County Herald*, January 11, 2002.

Fohn, Joe. "Cemetery recalls frontier times." *San Antonio Express*, April 2, 1982.

Graham, Don. "Wayne's World." *Texas Monthly*, March 2000.

Gutierrez-Mier, John. "'Alamo' Remembered Movie cast salutes 40th anniversary." *San Antonio Express-News*, September 7, 1999.

Hopper, Hedda. "'The Alamo' – A Dream Comes True For Duke." *San Antonio Express and News*, October 23, 1960.

Hopper, Heddy. "Looking at Hollywood – Movie-Men Shoot 'Alamo' in Mexico City." *San Antonio Express*, July 18, 1951.

Huddleston, Scott. "Alamo Village Closes Indefinitely." *San Antonio Express-News*, August 31, 2010.

———, "Then & Now: The other 'Alamo.'" *San Antonio Express-News*, March 7, 2004.

Jenkins, Leigh and Yvette Rocha. "Courthouse turns 100." *The Brackett News*, March 17, 2011.

Johnson, Erskine. "'Alamo' Set to be Tourist Mecca." *San Antonio Express*, October 28, 1959.

Kelton, Elmer. "They Built Another Alamo – Texans Lure Film Maker Wayne to Brackettville." *San Antonio Standard Times*, April 20, 1958.

Killin, Jennifer. "Set of 'The Alamo' closes to public." *Del Rio News-Herald*, July 5, 2009.

Kuykendall, Matt. "Mexicans 2 – Texans 0, Santa Anna Takes Rematch." *Unknown newspaper*, unknown date.

LaRoche, Clarence. "Brackettville – Country of the West." *San Antonio Light*, May 18, 1963.

Lemon, Mark. "Ramping Up the Scrutiny: The Most Probable Configuration of the Church Ramp." *The Alamo Journal*, December 2013.

———, "North Wall Revisited." *The Alamo Journal,* September 2012.

Lightman, Herb A. "Filming 'The Alamo' in Todd-AO." *American Cinematographer*, November 1960.

Lowe, Walter. "Hollywood Reconstructs Replica of The Alamo." *The Times Recorder*, December 23, 1959.

McDaniel, Ruel. "City Links Old and New Texas." *Dallas Morning News*, August 29, 1926.

Mousner, Jim. "The 2nd Alamo. Hollywood Spurs Quit Jingling, So Did Cash Register." *Houston Post*, June 12, 1960.

Nason, Richard. "Biggest Western To Cost $8,000,000." *The New York Times*, July 29, 1959.

Naughton, Walter. "Dies on Hollywood." *San Antonio Light*, June 29, 1944.

Norman, Jerry. "Brackettville Set Gains Applause From Movie." *San Angelo Standard Times*, September 1995.

Pickel, Don. "S.A. Movie Hope Revived." *San Antonio Light*, October 9, 1951.

Range, Rick. "North Wall Postscript." *The Alamo Journal*, December 2013.

Ratfliff, Larry. "A Texas treasure – John Wayne's 'Alamo' just part of the story for Texas' first film czar Happy Shahan." *San Antonio Express-News*, July 16, 1995.

Reeves, Frank. "New 'Old City' Astonishes Passersby." *Fort Worth Star Telegram*, March 22, 1959.

Roberts, Bill. "Dan Moody Plans $60,000 Apartment." *The Houston Post*, November 4, 1959.

Roselle, Ron. "One cold October night under a starry Texas sky." *The Facts*, October 15, 2006.

Scarbrough, Nina H. "Saga Of Alamo Is Being Re-enacted." *The Cuero Record*, November 1959.

Shanks, Dave. "Texas History Turns a Profit. Brackettville Is Claiming Fame." *The Austin American*, June 26, 1960.

Shannon, Kelley. "South Texas ranch set for Wild West." *Southwest Times*, September 15, 1991.

Sisk, Mack. "$4 million for an Alamo (but not for THE Alamo)." *San Antonio Express-News*, July 18, 1982.

Staff Writer. "Alamo Film to be Shot Near S.A." *San Antonio Express*, January 19, 1958.

———, "'Alamo' Office Burns Sunday." *Del Rio News-Herald*, November 16, 1959.

———, "The Alamo is Rising Anew." *Texas Co-op Power*, June 1958.

———, "Alamo Supplement." *San Antonio Express and News*, October 16, 1960.

———, "'Alamo Village' Future Unsure." *Victoria Advocate*, July 19, 1982.

———, "Alamo Village Open to Tourists." *San Antonio Light*, July 10, 1960.

———, "Alamo Village to celebrate 'The Duke's' birthday in style." *Del Rio News-Herald*, May 12, 1998.

―― ――, "'Alamo' winds Up 82-Day, $4 Mil Location; 1000 Horses On Block." *The Hollywood Reporter*, December 16, 1959.

―― ――, "Army Architecture." *The Fort Clark, Texas Post Return*, Winter, 2009, Vol. 2, No. 3, 3.

―― ――, "Battle of Alamo Over." *San Antonio Light*, December 15, 1959.

―― ――, "Body Pushes Battle For Alamo Plan." *San Antonio Light*, July 5, 1936.

―― ――, "Brackettville Builds Alamo." *San Antonio Light*, January 19, 1958.

―― ――, "Brackettville still has way to go on dream." *San Antonio Express-News*, December 21, 1980.

―― ――, "Chatterbox." *The Dallas News*, July 10, 1951.

―― ――, "Fire Destroys Fort of Wayne's Jinx Film." *Pasadena Independent*, November 16, 1959.

―― ――, "Fire Razes Fort Clark Film Site." *The Galveston News*, November 16, 1959.

―― ――, "Firm Has Alamo Village Sale." *Llano News*, April 26, 1973.

―― ――, "Has He Everything Now? How About the 'Alamo.'" *Houston Post*, October 20, 1971.

―― ――, "Heavy Rains Flood Roxton In Big Area Thunderstorm." *The Paris News*, June 17, 1958.

―― ――, "He's The Man Who Built Own Alamo." *San Antonio Express-News*, June 11, 1961.

―― ――, "Hollywood Stars Back Texas Town." *San Antonio Express and News*, August 19, 1961.

―― ――, "John Wayne's 'Alamo' Brings Hums Of Business to Brackettville." *San Antonio newspaper*, July 10, 1959.

―― ――, "Las Moras Creek Floods Brackett, Closing Highway 90 East Of Here." *Del Rio News-Herald*, June 17, 1958.

―― ――, "Lone Star Spread." *San Antonio Light*, December 29, 1958.

―― ――, "Movie Actors Play It Cool." *The Times-Picayune*, May 24, 1960.

―― ――, "New Thunderstorm Build Up As Nueces River Rises." *Big Spring Daily Herald*, June 18, 1958.

―― ――, "Rainfall Risk in Area May Be Reduced." *Del Rio News-Herald*, November 15, 1957.

―― ――, "Rains Drench Del Rio Area As Rio Grande, Devil's River Crest." *Del Rio News-Herald*, June 18, 1958.

―― ――, "Rancher Bill Moody Hurt As Horse Crashes Coach." *Unknown newspaper*, September 4, 1962.

―― ――, "Remembering the Alamo." *Del Rio News Herald*, May 15, 1998.

―― ――, "Rendering the Alamo." *American Heritage*, October/November 1979.

―― ――, "San Antonio Gets 'Rival.'" *San Antonio News*, January 16, 1959.

―― ――, "Shahan to sell Alamo Village." *Del Rio News-Herald*, July 18, 1982.

―― ――, "Shahan Will Sell For $2 Million." *San Antonio Express-News*, April 24, 1963.

―― ――, "Shooting of 'Alamo' in S.A. Unlikely." *San Antonio Light*, October 9, 1951.

―― ――, "Star, Producer Seek Texas Data." *San Antonio Light*, March 9, 1948.

―― ――, "Surprising Replica of Texas Liberty Shrine in New Locale. *Del Rio News-Herald*, March 1, 1959.

―― ――, "Wayne Takes On Texas." *San Antonio Light*, September 28, 1958.

―― ――, "Wet weather for most of nation." *Columbus Daily Telegram*, June 18, 1958.

Straach, Kathryn. "Brackettville reaches for the stars." *The Dallas Morning News*, September 10, 2000.

Tolbert, Frank X. "Border Scoured For 'Dobe Makers." *Dallas Morning News*, January 23, 1958.

———, "Brackettville Has Become a Sort Of Hollywood-on-Los-Moras-Creek." *San Antonio News*, November 12, 1967.

———, "When Chili Willie Came to Coahuila." *Dallas Morning News*, unknown date.

———, "Hollywood on the Rio." *Dallas Morning News*, April 16, 1961.

———, "Secret for Making Good Adobe Walls." *Dallas Morning News*, September 11, 1971.

Wagner, Bill. "Chapel of Alamo May Be Used for Forthcoming Film." *San Antonio Evening News*, October 8, 1951.

Walther, Ed. "Filming of 'The Alamo' Stardust to Brackettville Brings." *Daily Texan*, November 24, 1959.

Wilson, Charles Emily. "History of the Seminole Scout Cemetery." *The Brackett News*, September 18, 2008.

Winingham, Ralph. "Moviemakers to remember 'The Alamo.'" *San Antonio Express-News*, May 17, 1998.

Wynne, Robert. "Remember 'The Alamo' on its 30th anniversary." *San Antonio Light*, January 21, 1990.

Zaboly, Gary. "The Fall of William Barret Travis." *The Alamo Journal*, Sept. 2012.

Monograph/Pamphlets:

Dickman Hall, Kinney County Historical Commission RTHL, Monograph #19.

Kinney County Courthouse, Kinney County Historical Commission RTHL, Monograph # 12.

Kinney County Texas, Soldiers, Settles and Scouts, Kinney County Historical Commission, 2007.

New Cavalry Barracks/Seminole Hall, Kinney County Historical Commission RTHL, Monograph #17.

Original Town of Brackett Historic District, Kinney County Historic Commission, 2010.

Palisado Building-Kitchen/Messroom, Kinney County Historical Commission RTHL, Monograph #3.

Partrick Hotel, Kinney County Historical Commission RTHL, Monograph #16.

Recorded Texas Historic Landmarks in Kinney County, Kinney County Historical Commission, 2009.

U.S. Army Service Club, Kinney County Historical Commission RTHL, Monograph #18.

Script:

May 19, 1959

Miscellaneous:

Alamo Village map/brochure.
Alamo Village Story Boards, Rich Curilla.
Birdwell, Russell. "A News Release John Wayne's "The Alamo" (1960).
Master Shooting Schedule, August 21, 1959.
Ybarra, Al. Alamo chapel blueprint. March 1951.
—— ——, Alamo compound blueprint, undated.
—— ——, Alamo Village blueprint, undated.

Films/DVD:

Huberman, Brian. John Wayne Alamo documentary. MGM/UA, 1992.
"Spirit of the Alamo," The Pontiac Star Parade, November 14, 1960.

Internet:

www.ffchd.org
www.fortclark.com/history.html
www.geocities.com/the_tarins@sbcglobal.net/adp/archives/features/statues.html
www.homestead.com/alamovillagereunion/virginiashahan
www.johnwayne-thealamo.com (Alamo Village Brackettville, Immortal Alamo, June 24, 2009)
www.tamu.edu/faculty/ccbn/dewitt/dewitt.htm
www.texasbeyondhistory.net/forts.clark/saddle.html
www.tshaonline.org/handbook/online/articles/hjb14
www.tsha.utetax.edu/handbook/online/articles/view/FF/qbft10.html
www.tsl.state.tx.us/exhibits/parks/1950s/page1.html

Notes

1. *Hill Country Herald*, January 11, 2012; "Virginia Shahan." www.homestead.com/alamovillagereunion/virginiashahan; Jamie Shahan Rains to author, October 20, 2010.
2. www.tsl.state.tx.us/exhibits/parks/1950s/page1.html.
3. James Tullis "Happy" Shahan; *San Antonio Express-News*, July 16, 1995; Letter from/conversation with Richard Curilla; Texas Senate Concurrent Resolution No. 1112, April 12, 1995; *The Texas Mohair and Rocksprings Record*, May 27, 1960; Joe York, Jr. interview; Tully Shahan to author, October 21, 2010; ibid., November 18, 2010.
4. Bill Moody IV interview; Virginia Shahan interview; *San Antonio Light*, September 4, 1959; *This is West Texas*, November-December 1970, 20-23.
5. Chris Hale to author, July 1, 2015.
6. www.texasbeyondhistory.net; http://www.tamu.edu/faculty/ccbn/dewitt/dewitt.htm.
7. *The Fort Clark, Texas Post Return*, Winter 2009, Vol. 2, No. 3.
8. Caleb Pirtle III and Michael F. Cusack, *Fort Clark: The Lonely Sentinel On Texas's Western Frontier*, 13, 15, 17, 18.
9. ibid., 40-41.
10. ibid., 60-61.
11. www.fortclark.com/history.html; www.tsha.utetax.edu/handbook/online/articles/view/FF/qbft10.html; Steve Dial, "Empty Saddle at Mulberry Springs", www.texasbeyondhistory.net/forts.clark/saddle.html; *Brackett News Mail*, June 16, 1944; *Unknown newspaper*, July 26, 1970; William F. Haenn, *Fort Clark and Brackettville: Land of Heroes*, 7, 20.
12. *Recorded Texas Historic Landmarks in Kinney County*, Kinney County Historical Commission, 2009; *Original Town of Brackett Historic District*, Kinney County Historic Commission, 2010; *The Brackett News*, March 17, 2011; *Kinney County Texas, Soldiers, Settles and Scouts*, Kinney County Historical Commission, 2007.
13. *Kinney County Courthouse, Recorded Texas Historic Landmark 2003*, Kinney County Historical Commission, No. 12; *The Dallas News*, August 29, 1926; Pirtle and Cusack, 128.
14. Kinney County Texas, Soldiers, Settlers and Scouts, Kinney County Historical Commission, 2007.
15. Donald Clark and Christopher Andersen, *John Wayne's The Alamo. The Making of the Epic Film*, 16; Haenn, 108-9; *Daily Texan*, November 24, 1959; *San Antonio Light*, June 29, 1944; Ft Clark Springs visitor's pamphlet.

16. *San Antonio Light*, May 18, 1963; ibid., July 2, 1953; Pirtle and Cusack, 44, 78; *Brackett News*, March 17, 2011; *The Dallas News*, August 29, 1926; Haenn, 89; The *Dallas Morning News*, September 10, 2000; Ruben E. Ochoa, "BRACKETTVILLE, TX," *Handbook of Texas Online* (http://www.tshaonline.org/handbook/online/articles/hjb14), accessed June 06, 2015. Uploaded on June 12, 2010. Published by the Texas State Historical Association. Agnes Fritter, "Pioneer Days of Kinney County," *Texas History Teachers Bulletin* 13 (1946). *Kinney County: 125 Years of Growth, 1852–1977* (Brackettville, Texas: Kinney County Historical Society, 1977). Vertical Files, Dolph Briscoe Center for American History, University of Texas at Austin.
17. Ron Field, U.S. A*rmy Frontier Scouts 1840-1921*, 41; *Dallas Morning News*, August 29, 1926; *San Antonio Express-News*, April 2, 1982; *San Antonio News*, November 12, 1967; April 2, 1982; Haenn, 6, 30; www.ffchd.org; Seminole-Negro Indian Scout Camp, Kinney Coun*ty Historical Commission*, 2007; *The Brackett News*, September 18, 2008.
18. David Rothel, *An Ambush of Ghosts*, 14; B.J. Burns interview; *Austin American Statesman*, May 29, 1977; Happy Shahan interview, FTC; *San Antonio Express*, October 26, 1952; Moody IV interview.
19. Moody IV interview; *San Antonio Standard Times*, April 20, 1958; *Houston Post*, June 12, 1960; *San Antonio Express-News*, June 11, 1961; ibid., September 16, 1989; Curilla interview; *Austin American Statesman*, May 29, 1977; *Dallas Morning News*, September 10, 2000.
20. Frank Thompson, *Texas Hollywood-Filmmaking in San Antonio since 1910*, 50; *San Antonio Standard Times*, April 20, 1958; Hedda Hopper, "Hedda Hopper's Hollywood," press release, January 23, 1960; Chuck Roberson with Bodie Thoene, *The Fall Guy: 30 Years as Duke's Double*, 230; *San Antonio Express-News,* October, 1959.
21. *Los Angeles Examiner*, May 7, 1958.
22. Virginia Shahan interview; *San Antonio Express-News*, July 16, 1995; Curilla; Randy Roberts and James S. Olson, *John Wayne–American* , 457; *Austin American Statesman*, May 29, 1977: Clark and Andersen, 12-13.
23. *Texas Highways*, May 1985, 37; Brian Huberman, "John Wayne's *The Alamo*," MGM, 1992, Happy Shahan interview; Curilla; *San Antonio Express-News*, September 16, 1989.
24. *Texas Monthly*, March 2000, 108.
25. Herb Fagen, *Duke–We're Glad We Knew You*, 128; *San Antonio Express*, March 9, 10, 1948; ibid., July 18, 1951; Michael Munn, *John Wayne–The Man Behind the Myth*,131; *Dallas Morning News*, July 10, 1951; Letter from R.J. O'Donnell to Herbert Yates, June 21, 1951.
26. *San Antonio Light*, October 9, 10, 1951; *San Antonio Express*, October 9, 1951; *San Antonio Evening News*, October 8, 1951; Clark and Andersen, 18.
27. Munn, 151; Pilar Wayne with Alex Thorliefson, *John Wayne: My Life with the Duke*, 59; Roberts and Olson, 383-84, 338-9; Aissa Wayne with Steve Delsohn, *John Wayne My Father*, 12; Donald Shepherd and Robert Slatzer, *Duke: The Life and Times of John Wayne*, 190, 204; *San Antonio Express News*, October 16, 1960.
28. Huberman, Shahan interview; *San Antonio Express-News*, July 16, 1995, May 17, 1998; Frank Thompson, *Alamo Movies*, 68; *The Cuero Record*, November 1959.
29. Curilla; Thompson, *Alamo Movies*, 68.
30. Happy Shahan interview, TTU.
31. *Austin American Statesman*, May 29, 1977; Happy Shahan interview, TTU.

32. *Out on the Land*, season 5, episode 62, "John Wayne's The Alamo movie set on the Shahan ranch."
33. Happy Shahan interview, TTU.
34. ibid., Curilla.
35. Mary Hernandez to author, undated; *Texas Highways*, May 1985, 37; Happy Shahan interview, TTU.
36. Jose Hernandez III interview; Margarita Talmantez to author, undated; Margarita Talmantez interview; Jose Hernandez III to author May 25, 2004.
37. Jose Hernandez III interview; Mary Hernandez interview; *Texas Highways*, May 1985, 36-43; Happy Shahan interview, FTC; Rothel, 15.
38. Thompson, *Alamo Movies*, 68-70; Russell Birdwell, "A News Release John Wayne's "The Alamo" (1960), 92-93; Curilla; *Southwest Times*, September 15, 1991; Clark and Anderson, 28; *San Antonio Express*, January 19, 1958; Ronald L. Davis, *Duke: The Life and Image of John Wayne*, 222; Moody IV interview.
39. *Texas Highways*, May, 1985, 36-43.
40. *Dallas Morning News*, March 26, 1958; *The Kinney County News*, January 17, 1958; *The Houston Chronicle*, October 15, 1958; *Unknown newspaper*, mid-December 1958; *San Antonio Express and News*, March 15, 1959; *Unknown newspaper*, unknown date; Curilla; *Texas Highways*, May 1985.
41. Rich Curilla to author, March 25, 2011; ibid,. April 5, 2011; Al Ybarra, FTC; Al Ybarra blueprint of Alamo and village, undated.
42. Ybarra interview, FTC.
43. Happy Shahan interview, TTU.
44. *San Antonio Standard-Times*, April 20, 1958; *San Antonio Light*, September 28; ibid., December 29, 1958; *San Antonio Express-News*, October 16, 1960; Measurements taken from Styrofoam block in author's possession; Ralph Gonzales interview; *The Dallas Morning News*, September 11, 1971; ibid., January 23, 1958; *San Antonio News*, January 16, 1959; *The Times Recorder*, December 23, 1959.
45. *The Columbus Daily Telegram*, June 18, 1958; *Big Spring Herald*, June 18, 1958; *Del Rio News-Herald*, June 18, 1958; ibid., June 17, 1958; *The Paris News*, June 17, 1958.
46. Ybarra interview, FTC; *Del Rio News-Herald*, November 15, 1957; *The Dallas Morning News*, unknown date.
47. Gonzales interview; *The Dallas Morning News*, September 11, 1971; ibid., January 23, 1958; *San Antonio News*, January 16, 1959; *The Times Recorder*, December 23, 1959.
48. Pirtle and Cusack, 167-170.
49. *The Kinney County News*, January 17, 1958; *Texas Co-op Power*, June 1958; *Del Rio News-Herald*, unknown date.
50. Alan Kreiger, Jr. interview.
51. *San Antonio Express*, January 19, 1958; *Unknown newspaper*, unknown date; USC, John Wayne collection, box 3, folder 2, Bank of America loan agreement with Batjac dated May 25, 1960.
52. ibid.,;*The Cuero Record*, November, 1959; *San Antonio Express*, January 19, 1958; Roberts and Olson, 462; *San Antonio Light*, December, 1959; *The Kinney County News*, January 17, 1958; *Texas Co-op Power*, June 1958, 4; *Del Rio Herald*, unknown date; Kreiger, Jr. interview; *San Antonio Express*, January 19, 1958; *Unknown newspaper*, unknown date.

53. Henry Fuentes interview.
54. Susan Prendergast Schoelwer, *Alamo Images – Changing Perceptions of a Texas Experience,* 25; Curilla; *Rio Grande Review,* February, 1959; *San Antonio Standard-Times,* April 20, 1958; *San Antonio Light,* January 19, 1958; ibid., July 16, 1959; Todd Hansen, *The Alamo Reader–A Study in History,* 740.
55. Curilla; *San Antonio Light,* July 5, 1936; Birdwell, 93.
56. "Spirit of the Alamo," The Pontiac Star Parade November, 14, 1960; Curilla; May 19, 1959 script; Birdwell, 93; Schoelwer, 21; Elaine Davis to author September 26, 2003; ibid., June 9, 2004.
57. Curilla; author's photo collection and Ybarra original construction drawing, Set # 11, EXT. Alamo.
58. *Austin American-Statesman,* June 26, 1960.
59. Curilla.
60. Herbert G. Uecker, *The Archaeology of the Alamo*; Alan C. Hufines, *Blood of Noble Men,*122-127; *The Alamo Journal,* Sept. 2012; *The Alamo Journal,* Dec. 2013; Hansen, 570-597; Mark Lemon, *The Illustrated Alamo 1836,* 22-24, 58-9, 68, 71.
61. "The Search for the Saints," James Ivey, James Crisp, Kevin Young & John Bryant. www.geocities.com/the_tarins@sbcglobal.net/adp/archives/features/statues.html; *American Heritage,* October/November 1979, 50; Thompson, *Alamo Movies,* 72; Ybarra interview, FTC; Clark and Andersen, 41-42.
62. Clark and Andersen, 33; Chuck Schoenfeld to author, November 8, 2012; Don Clark to author, April 25, 2011; Ybarra construction drawings.
63. Uecker, 26; Curilla.
64. *The Alamo Journal,* December, 2013.
65. Curilla; *San Antonio Light,* November 14, 1958.
66. Uecker, 40; Huffines, 126; Curilla; Ybarra construction drawings; Lemon, 82.
67. ibid., 82.
68. Tim Cumiskey interview; Ybarra interview, FTC; *San Antonio Standard Times,* April 20, 1958; *Fort Worth Star Telegram,* March 22, 1959; Clark and Andersen, 40; Scott Eyman, *John Wayne: The Life and Legend,* 311; ibid., 319; *San Antonio Light,* December 29, 1958; *Del Rio News-Herald,* March 1, 1959.
69. Conversation between Al Ybarra and Ken Pruitt related to author June 25, 2005; Curilla history boards, Alamo Village; *San Antonio Standard-Times,* April 20, 1958; Clark and Andersen, 32.
70. *San Antonio Light,* mid to late 1958.
71. *San Antonio Light,* November 14, 1958.
72. Curilla; Virginia Shahan interview; *San Antonio Express-News,* October 23, 1960; Munn, 204; Happy Shahan interview, TTU; Curilla to author, March 25 through 28, 2013.
73. *San Antonio Light,* mid to late 1958; Pilar Wayne, 141.
74. *San Antonio Light,* December 29, 1958; Birdwell, 94-95; *San Antonio newspaper,* July 10, 1959; Curilla and author's visual confirmation.
75. Curilla; Alamo Village map/brochure.
76. *San Antonio Light,* mid to late 1958; Curilla; May 19, 1959 Script.
77. *Dallas Morning News,* December 12, 1959; *San Antonio Light,* December 15, 1959; *Del Rio News-Herald,* March 1, 1959; *Hollywood Reporter,* December 16, 1959; *The Times*

Recorder, December 23, 1959; *The Times-Picayune*, May 24, 1960.
78. *San Antonio Light*, November 4, 1958; Curilla to author, June 16, 2014; B.J. Burns interview.
79. *San Angelo Standard Times*, September 1995; *The Houston Post*, November 4, 1959; *San Antonio Light*, July 16, 1959; *New York Times*, July 29,1959; ibid., October 4, 1959; *San Antonio Express and News*, August 23, 1959; Munn, 204.
80. Ybarra interview, FTC; Clark and Andersen, 41-2.
81. Jose Hernandez III interview; Visual comparison of before and after photos in author's collection.
82. Curilla; Clark and Anderson, 80.
83. John Farkis, *Not Thinkin'…Just Rememberin'…" The Making of John Wayne's The Alamo*, 457-61.
84. Moody IV interview; Curilla.
85. Farkis, 457; Crystal Harvey Wade interview.
86. Chuck Hall interview.
87. *American Cinematographer*, November, 1960, 662-63, 699-700, 702; Plunker Sheedy interview; Robert Relyea interview; *San Antonio Light*, September 4, 1959; Robert Harris interview; Robert Relyea, *Not So Quiet On The Set: My Life in Movies During Hollywood's Macho Era*, 121-22.
88. Curilla.
89. Lightman, 699; Curilla.
90. Farkis, 443; Curilla.
91. Curilla and author's observation.
92. Farkis, 511-12; Thompson, 77; Rudy Robbins to author, October 10, 12, 2006; *San Antonio Express and News*, October 23, 1960; *The Alamo Journal*, June 2007.
93. Rudy Robbins interview.
94. Clark and Andersen, 88-9; Haenn, 124; *The Fort Clark, Texas Post Return*, Winter 2009, Vol. 2, No. 3, 3.
95. *The Fort Clark, Texas Post Return*, Vol. 2, No. 1, Sumer 2008; Robert Relyea to author, May 5, 2010; ibid., May 11, 2010; *The Galveston News*, November 16, 1959; *Pasadena Independent*, November 16, 1959; *Del Rio News-Herald*, November 16, 1959.
96. Curilla; Curilla to author, March 25 through 28, 2013.
97. *San Antonio Light*, November 1959; *San Antonio Express-News*, October 23, 1960; ibid., July 16, 1995; Virginia Shahan interview; *Dallas Morning News*, October 8, 1961.
98. *Unkown newspaper*, June 4, 1980.
99. *San Antonio Light*, mid to late 1958; *Houston Chronicle*, October 15, 1958.
100. *Austin American Statesman*, May 29, 1977; *San Antonio Light*, July 10, 1960; *San Antonio Express*, October 28, 1959.
101. *San Antonio Light*, July 10, 1960.
102. Curilla; Alamo Village history boards; *San Antonio Express-News*, December 21, 1980.
103. *Dallas News*, April 16, 1961; September, 1961 proposed contract between MasterCraft and Happy Shahan; *San Antonio Light*, May 18, 1963.
104. *San Antonio Light*, May 18, 1963; *San Antonio Express-News*, December 21, 1980; *The Dallas Morning News*, October 8, 1961.
105. *San Antonio Express and News*, August 19, 1961.

106. *San Antonio Light*, 1962; *Unknown newspaper*, September 4, 1962.
107. *Austin American Statesman*, May 29, 1977.
108. *Houston Post*, October 20, 1971; *San Antonio Express News*, April 24, 1963.
109. *Llano News*, April 26, 1973; *The Day*, January 31, 1975; *Fort Worth Star Telegram*, April 27, 1976; *News-Sentinel*, January 28, 1975; *Chicago Tribune*, January 24, 1975.
110. Ad, *San Antonio Express*, August 29, 1977.
111. *San Antonio Express-News*, July 18, 1982; *Del Rio News-Herald*, July 18, 1982; *Victoria Advocate*, July 19, 1982.
112. *San Antonio Express-News*, September 16, 1989; *The Dallas Morning News*, September 10, 2000.
113. *San Antonio Express-News*, July 16, 1995.
114. www.johnwayne-thealamo.com, "Alamo Village Brackettville, Virginia Shahan Passes, Immortal Alamo," June 24, 2009; *The Brackett News*, June 25, 2009.
115. Public notice, Alamo reunion, May 23-24, 1998; *Del Rio News-Herald*, May 12, 1998; ibid., May 15, 1998.
116. *Unknown newspaper*, unknown date.
117. *San Antonio Express-News*, March 7, 2004; *The Facts (Brazos)*, October 15, 2006; *New York Times,* March 26, 2004.
118. *Del Rio News-Herald*, July 5, 2009.
119. *The Brackett News*, September 9, 2010.
120. *San Antonio Express News*, August 31, 2010.
121. *New Cavalry Barracks/Seminole Hall*, Kinney County Historical Commission RTHL, Monograph #17.
122. *Dickman Hall*, Kinney County Historical Commission RTHL, Monograph #19.
123. *Palisado Building-Kitchen/Messroom,* Kinney County Historical Commission RTHL, Monograph #3.
124. *Recorded Texas Historic Landmarks in Kinney County,* Kinney County Historical Commission, 2009.
125. *U.S. Army Service Club*, Kinney County Historical Commission RTHL, Monograph #18.
126. *Kinney County Courthouse*, Kinney County Historical Commission RTHL, Monograph # 12.
127. *Recorded Texas Historic Landmarks in Kinney County*, Kinney County Historical Commission, 2009.
128. *Partrick Hotel*, Kinney County Historical Commission RTHL, Monograph #16.

www.ingramcontent.com/pod-product-compliance
Lightning Source LLC
Chambersburg PA
CBHW080535170426
43195CB00016B/2571